A WOMAN'S RIGHT TO CULTURE

A WOMAN'S RIGHT TO CULTURE

TOWARD GENDERED CULTURAL RIGHTS

by

Linda L. Veazey

ЧP

QUID PRO BOOKS

New Orleans, Louisiana

Published in 2015 by Quid Pro Books.

ISBN 978-1-61027-314-5 (pbk)
ISBN 978-1-61027-329-9 (hc)
ISBN 978-1-61027-315-2 (eBook)

QUID PRO BOOKS

5860 Citrus Blvd., Suite D-101
New Orleans, Louisiana 70123
www.quidprobooks.com

qp

Publisher's Cataloging-in-Publication

Veazey, Linda L.
    A Woman's Right to Culture: Toward Gendered Cultural Rights / Linda L. Veazey.
        p. cm. — (Dissertation series)
    Includes bibliographical references.
    ISBN 978-1-61027-314-5 (paperback)
1. Sex role—Cross-cultural studies. 2. Women's rights—Cross-cultural studies. 3. Social
change—Cross-cultural studies. I. Title. II. Series.
HQ1073.V13 2015   2015469871

Cover image courtesy NASA Johnson Space Center, Gateway to Astronaut Photography of
Earth (Dec. 7, 1972): "View of the Earth as seen by the Apollo 17 crew traveling toward
the moon." Author photograph on back cover inset provided courtesy of Jennifer Conklin,
used by permission. Cover design © 2015 by Quid Pro, LLC.

CONTENTS

FOREWORD

This unusual book, *A Woman's Right to Culture: Toward Gendered Cultural Rights*, provides a novel interpretation of women's human rights. This superb monograph written by political scientist and human rights advocate Dr. Linda Veazey is cutting-edge research in sociolegal scholarship concerning the status of global feminism.

In this engaging study of feminist jurisprudence from across the globe, Veazey examines the interrelationship among women's rights, cultural rights, and religious freedom through a set of compelling case studies about dress codes, family law (marriage and divorce, and child custody), and indigenous rights to land. Veazey advances the perhaps somewhat surprising argument that women's rights and other rights are not necessarily in opposition, but actually may be mutually reinforcing, at least in some circumstances.

One case study focuses on the French controversy about the headscarf (which continued as in the European Court of Human Rights decision, *S.A.S. v. France* (2014); the Court, with unconvincing reasoning, upheld the burqa ban in public places on the ground that the ban promoted "vivre ensemble" or living together harmoniously). Another provocative chapter examines the Hindmarsh Bridge Island Affair litigation, involving an Australian aboriginal conflict over a sacred site on an island ostensibly used for "secret women's business." Each chapter contains an incisive analysis of a controversy that illuminates an aspect of the interrelationship between women's rights and cultural rights. After providing the context for the litigation, Veazey delves into the specific rights claims at the crux of the matter. From these captivating chapters that provide detailed legal histories from around the world, the reader learns to appreciate the challenges associated with empowering women in differing social contexts.

Her subtle interpretation of the complex relationship between women's rights and cultural rights is of great interest partly because she challenges the view of the late feminist scholar Susan Moller Okin. Okin's well-known position that women's rights and cultural rights are necessarily in opposition, found in *Is Multiculturalism Bad for Women?* (1999), has received much attention. Veazey demonstrates convincingly the fallacy in Okin's argument through her series of case studies. By dissecting the

i

competing rights claims at the crux of specific controversies, Veazey shows that a much more nuanced treatment of human rights standards is required. Instead of assuming that cultural rights invariably undermine women's rights, she proves that women, at times, wish to remain in their communities, even if they are patriarchal societies. Women find strength in a sense of belonging, and seek empowerment, so they can bring about significant social change. A better strategy for women's rights may be to support their efforts to effect meaningful change from within societies, instead of focusing almost exclusively on the right of exit and methods of exerting pressuring from outside. This book is full of thought-provoking examples that support her main argument.

Within the United Nations there has long been a tendency to avoid addressing the relationships between and among specific human rights. For instance, the *Convention on the Elimination of All Forms of Discrimination against Women* (CEDAW), in Articles 2(f) and 5, prohibits traditions that violate women's rights. However, the International Covenant on Civil and Political Rights guarantees the right to culture including religious liberty in Article 27, and the latter contains no restrictions clause. It is worth noting that many states are parties to both of these treaties, so it is crucial to think through the relative prioritization of women's rights and cultural rights! Consequently, greater attention should certainly be paid to identifying specific traditions that result in irreparable harm, in order to distinguish between harmful cultural traditions and innocuous ones. It is also important to empower those within cultural communities to make desired changes rather than imposing the changes from abroad. The UN special rapporteur on Traditions Harmful to Women and Child lists specific customs deemed harmful without providing any analysis or interpretation,[1] as does the UN special rapporteur on Violence Against Women.[2] The UN special rapporteur in the field of Cultural Rights has acknowledged the tension[3] but does not provide an analytic framework for

---

[1] See the reports by Halima Embarek Warzazi on "Traditional Practices Affecting the Health of Women and the Girl Child," e.g., http://www.refworld.org/docid/3f4f81ob4.html (July 2, 2002).

[2] The reader may also wish to consult reports of the UN special rapporteur on Violence Against Women, http://www.ohchr.org/EN/Issues/Women/SRWomen/Pages/SRWomenIndex.aspx.

[3] Fareeda Shaheed, the first UN special rapporteur in the field of Cultural Rights, issued a statement in 2012 that notes the complex interrelationship, though this was not a focus of her investigations during her six-year tenure. But see her twenty-four-page report, http://www.ohchr.org/EN/Issues/CulturalRights/Pages/Culturalrightsofwomen.aspx.

making this distinction.[4] To date, there has been relatively little effort to reconcile the tensions in human rights standards that are part of the "hierarchy" challenge. Veazey's manuscript takes a step in this direction by disentangling claims in specific circumstances. It provides an exemplar for future human rights scholars. She shows convincingly that scholars and advocates must take greater care in analyzing policy debates in the light of competing international human rights claims.

In her engaging work, Veazey makes an important contribution to legal theory, public law, feminist studies, political science, and human rights scholarship. Her fascinating analysis of the interrelationship between women's rights and cultural rights will undoubtedly be considered a classic. There is simply no book like it.

ALISON DUNDES RENTELN
Professor of Political Science,
Anthropology, Law, and Public Policy
University of Southern California

Los Angeles, California
September 2015

---

[4] Consider Chia Longman and Tamsin Bradley (Eds.) (2015). *Interrogating Harmful Cultural Practices: Gender, Culture and Coercion.* Burlington, VT: Ashgate Publishing Co.

PREFACE

"Women's Rights are Human Rights," the slogan went—as women's rights scholars and activists sought for full inclusion in human rights discourse of the challenges women face in invoking their rights. At the United Nations and within human rights organizations, the issue has moved on to gender mainstreaming, to ensure that women's rights are part of all aspects of human rights work. However, one aspect of human rights that has not received full integration with women's rights is the right to culture. Cultural rights and women's rights are often seen as contradictory. In balancing the many and sometimes competing human rights enshrined in international law, the rights of individuals are often pitted against those of the group and the protection of the rights of women pitted against the rights of the culture.

Furthermore, the women's human rights literature often takes as its premise the protection of individual women's rights against patriarchal communities. Women's human rights scholarship centers on the *Convention on the Elimination of All Forms of Discrimination against Women* (CEDAW), which attempts to address the particular legal and cultural barriers women face in accessing their human rights; the treaty and this scholarship tend to view culture as the enemy to be vanquished. While the Convention should be applauded as a valiant attempt at codification, it reflects a Western bias towards the individual and presumes that culture is necessarily patriarchal. Culture is often vilified as something from which women should be liberated. Gender and culture are automatically assumed to stand in opposition to one another.

However, when examining actual cases of rights conflicts involving gender and culture, the reality women face is more complex. Gender and culture are not so easily separated because all persons exist within a particular cultural context. Making women's liberation contingent on the shedding of culture holds non-Western women to a double standard, and unduly defines culture in negative and patriarchal terms. This approach then denies women the existence of women's culture and casts women as victims of their societies rather than as active participants within them.

The relationship between women's rights and the right to culture is complex. However, human rights instruments, scholars, organizations, and activists have not focused on the relationship between women's rights and cultural rights, except in a negative context. When these rights are pitted against each other in an adversarial manner, rights concerns are oversimplified and women are forced to choose a single label for their rights concerns, one which may be ill-suited. I propose that women have cultural rights, but to fully recognize this, neither the current conception of women's rights or cultural rights is adequate.

Rights can be mutually reinforcing instead of mutually exclusive. Invoking women's human rights does not necessarily lead to the destruction of culture. The multilayered identity of women, especially in the Western, multicultural state, requires a reimagining of culture in which women's roles and traditions are seen as cultural contributions that have the potential capacity for empowerment in both the public and private spheres. I argue for a new category of gendered cultural rights that recognizes the relationship between gender rights and cultural rights, allowing for additional avenues to address human rights concerns.

Examining rights conflicts through the lens of gendered cultural rights, I have chosen to explore disputes in which, on the surface, women's human rights appear at odds with the right to culture. Applying research techniques from legal anthropology, I examine several rights conflicts that affect women's participation in both their communities and the larger society. Legal disputes such as the debate over the hijab in France, divorce in Orthodox Judaism in the U.S. and Canada, adoption in the U.S. Indian Child Welfare Act, and the Hindmarsh Island Bridge Affair in South Australia pull the focus of the examination of women and culture toward the more subtle debates arising in society. Through a careful analysis of several case studies, I demonstrate the need for a reconceptualization of the nature of women's cultural rights. Ultimately, I explore the theoretical implications and policy implications of gendered cultural rights. This new category of gendered cultural rights, if institutionalized, may offer new solutions to social problems.

This book is based on my original study, prepared as part of the requirements for my Ph.D. degree in political science from the University of Southern California in May 2008. Although it is adapted for the present and edited and updated for publication as a book, there are certainly some recent sources and observations that I would have preferred to have updated as well. This project, though, is included in the Dissertation Series, which asks the author to preserve as much as possible of the original research and structure for readers and researchers, rather than attempting to create a thoroughly revised narrative, and therefore I left some thoughts and phrasings frozen in the perspective of the late 2000s. However, I am struck on re-reading by how much of the narrative remains true today. I hope it proves useful in published form to readers, students, and researchers in the field.

LINDA L. VEAZEY
Assistant Professor of Political Science, and
Program Coordinator of Women's and Gender Studies
Midwestern State University

Wichita Falls, Texas
October 2015

ACKNOWLEDGMENTS

This book would not have been possible without the wonderful guidance and support of Professor Alison Dundes Renteln. My sincere gratitude to her as my mentor and professor. Many thanks, as well, are due Professor Janelle Wong and Professor Bettine Birge as members of my dissertation committee. Additionally, I would like to thank Professor Nancy Luktehaus for her excellent feedback on my work. To Professor Scott Turner, thank you for helping me to dream this possibility. To the Women's and Gender Studies Program at the University of Houston and Professor Elizabeth Gregory, the postdoctoral fellowship I received there was helpful in guiding me.

My colleagues at Midwestern State University have been immensely supportive of my work and I thank them for that. Thank you to Annette and Clark Veazey, whose support has allowed me to take this journey. To Archana Agarwal, Donald Bierer, Holle Canatella, Heather Edwards, Randa Issa, Jinee Lokaneeta, Alvis Minor, Kathy Hansen, Elizabeth Suarez, Alice Villaseñor, and Jason Whitehead, thank you for suggestions, but even more for your friendship and support. To Lee Scheingold, senior editor at Quid Pro Books, for her helpful questions and suggestions. Most of all, thank you to my husband, Drew Conklin, for his unwavering support and love.

L.L.V.

A Woman's Right to Culture

1

INTRODUCTION

In 1977 the Human Rights Committee, the treaty body of the *International Covenant on Civil and Political Rights* (ICCPR), heard Sandra Lovelace's complaint that Canada had violated the international treaty by allowing the Maliseet people to revoke her membership. She had married a non-member and, according to the rules of her indigenous community, thereby lost her own tribal membership and the corresponding cultural identity. This was not true of men marrying outside the tribe. By the time her case reached the Human Rights Committee (HRC), she had ceased to be a member of her tribe and hence was not a minority whose cultural rights had been denied.[1] The treaty body managed to sidestep the issue of membership rules in order to address the new question before them: should Lovelace be allowed to rejoin her people as a member? The Human Rights Committee held that Lovelace had a right to be part of her culture.[2]

This case is a landmark in international human rights because it recognizes the importance of the right to culture. There have been subsequent cases on this subject, and numerous scholars have weighed in on this right. However, something has been lost in that literature: women. Sandra Lovelace brought her complaint against Canada because this multicultural, Western state had a responsibility under international law to balance the rights of individuals and groups within society. Nowhere in the literature on international law, human rights, or political theory is there any direct treatment of women's human right to culture. It is this overlooked question that I take up in order to argue for gendered cultural rights.

In balancing the many and sometimes contradictory human rights enshrined in international law, the rights of individuals are often pitted against those of the group and the rights of women pitted against the rights of the culture. Furthermore, the women's human rights literature, consisting of predominantly Western works, takes as its premise the protection of individual women's rights against patriarchal communities. Women's

---

[1] *Sandra Lovelace v. Canada*. Communication No. R.6/24. Views of the Human Rights Committee. Report of the Human Rights Committee, Annex XVIII. General Assembly Official Records, 36th Session, Supplement No. 40 (A/36/40). New York: United Nations, 1981.

[2] Ibid.

1

human rights scholarship centers on the *Convention on the Elimination of All Forms of Discrimination against Women* (CEDAW). As a treaty which attempts to address the legal and cultural barriers women face in accessing their human rights, this Convention tends to view culture as the enemy to be vanquished. While the treaty is a valiant attempt at codification, it reflects a Western bias towards the individual in its presumption that culture is necessarily patriarchal. Culture is vilified as something from which women should be liberated. Gender and culture are automatically assumed to be in opposition to one another.

When examining actual cases of rights conflicts involving gender and culture, the reality of women's conditions is not so simple. Gender and culture are not easily separated, because all persons exist within a particular cultural context. Implicit in the argument that Western feminists and women's human rights scholars make against culture is the assumption that only those living outside of Western, industrialized nations have "culture." Therefore, the contingency of women's liberation on the shedding of culture holds non-Western women to a double standard, and defines culture solely in negative and patriarchal terms. This stance denies women the existence of women's culture and paints women as permanent victims of their societies.

In order to study this phenomenon, I engage in a textual analysis of cases involving these issues, identifying cases in which a tension exists between women's rights and the right to culture. These cases may appear to support the argument that gender and culture are at odds, but when they are probed in depth, a complex interrelationship between gender and culture is revealed. Applying methods from legal anthropology, I use the extended case method to investigate cross-culturally a legal controversy in the contemporary multicultural state. Detailed analysis of the cases allows me to examine the use of law in the particular social context of the case and its theoretical implications.[3] I explore the complexities of issues which are often oversimplified in the discourses of feminist theory and human rights, in order to argue for a category of gendered cultural rights.

Gender vs. Culture in Popular Culture

Rights conflicts are not limited to academic discourse. Human rights organizations, international bodies, nation-states, and the media contribute to both the philosophical and popular understanding of human rights. Although all of these play important roles in shaping human rights agen-

---

[3] J. van Velsen (1967). "The Extended-case Method and Situational Analysis." In A. L. Epstein (Ed.), *The Craft of Social Anthropology*. London: Tavistock, pp. 129-149.

das, the media is of particular importance in shaping the public perception of rights and rights conflicts, especially those discussing gender and culture.

For more than a decade, honor killings and female genital mutilation, commonly known as FGM, have been the main issues in the media associated with conflicts between gender and culture. While these practices are completely different, both serve as examples in Western media outlets of creating a discourse in which the relationship between gender and cultural rights is clear: culture is deadly to women. Western feminists such as Andrea Dworkin and Mary Daly use these examples to support the theory of the universal violence women face. They see culture as inherently patriarchal. Daly contends that women's oppression is universal, and any defense of these aspects of culture is anti-woman. However, Daly's choices of cultural practices in her discussion reflect her bias. She chooses to highlight practices such as FGM in non-Western societies that Westerners find particularly offensive.[4] Implicit in her argument is the assumption that women must be liberated from culture, but her choice of examples shows that she seeks to rescue only non-Western women. Like Dworkin, Daly seems both fascinated and enraged by the details of the practices. Resembling other works in both feminism and human rights, she has continued to promulgate this view of women's relationship to culture.[5]

This cultural practice of FGM, for example, occurs in many parts of Africa and is performed for many reasons by women themselves. The act of female genital cutting is hotly debated as a cultural right or an affront to individual autonomy. It is performed to ensure a woman will stay a virgin until her marriage, and it also signals a woman's readiness for marriage and adulthood.[6] It can cause extreme physical harm if not done safely, but for a woman to reject this practice would be to reject her entire culture and community.[7] "It is believed that uncircumcised women are more likely to

---

[4] Mary Daly (1978). *Gyn/ecology: The Metaethics of Radical Feminism*. Boston: Beacon Press, p. 4. Daly discusses footbinding in China as an example of the harmful effect of culture on women. Dorothy Ko reexamines footbinding as a convention of womanhood for some women. See Dorothy Ko (2005). *Cinderella's Sisters*. Berkeley; Los Angeles: University of California Press.

[5] Daly, supra n4, p. 6.

[6] December Green (1999). *Gender Violence in Africa: African Women's Responses*. New York: St. Martin's Press, p. 49.

[7] Leslye Ameda Obiora takes a middle ground on this debate. She suggests that allowing for the "medicalization" of the female circumcision could defuse the debate, because women would be protected from extremely harmful practices. However, reformers have fought this move because it would legitimate the practice. See Leslye Ameda Obiora (1997). "Bridges and

be unruly and promiscuous, and women who have undergone this ceremony have been educated in the appropriate role of a wife."[8] This is a cultural practice that women help to perpetuate. Of course, the custom has the blessing of the men in the community, but it has become a significant rite of passage.

However, the discussion of FGM and other similar issues popularized in the Western media distorts the terms of the debate by highlighting instances of conflict between the individual rights of women and cultural practice. These news stories come from Africa and the Middle East and fit into a broader Western stereotype of the developing world. Discussions of cultural traditions are often reduced to FGM and similar practices against which scholars and activists, especially in the West, can unite.[9] This overwhelming emphasis on certain traditions can perpetuate notions of Western cultural imperialism.[10] The Western and non-Western world seem diametrically opposed in the news media's presentation of human rights issues.[11] The project of women's liberation from cultural practice carries with it a subtext of Western cultural imperialism, when examined in this context.

My goal in this project is not to defend honor killings or FGM, but to point out the bias of the debate. I do not deny the grave human rights concerns these customs pose. The test should come, though, from the desires of the women of the community. I focus on the more subtle conflicts that arise between Western individualistic conceptions of women's rights and the conventional interpretations of group rights, particularly in the Western, multicultural state. While Western states are based upon

---

Barricades: Rethinking Polemics and Intransigence in the Campaign against Female Circumcision." In Adrien Katherine Wing (Ed.) (2000). *Global Critical Race Feminism*, pp. 260-274.

[8] Supra n6.

[9] Gender and culture are depicted as being in opposition and the discussion of cultural practices and gender is often a discussion of FGM, a harmful cultural practice. See David Weissbrodt and Connie de la Vega (2007). *International Human Rights Law: An Introduction*. Philadelphia: University of Pennsylvania Press.

[10] See Corinne Packer. "African Women, Traditions, and Human Rights: A Critical Analysis of Contemporary 'Universal' Discourses and Approaches." In David P. Forsythe and Patrice C. McMahon (Eds.). *Human Rights and Diversity: Area Studies Revisited.*

[11] Many postcolonial and third-world feminists have directly criticized the work of Mary Daly on this point, because her work depicted non-Western women needing Western saviors. Concerns and experience of non-Western women does not inform her work except to further the narrative of the harm that culture does to women. For a critique of Daly, see Kwok Pui-lan (2002), "Unbinding Our Feet: Saving Brown Women and Feminist Religious Discourse," in Laura E. Donaldson and Kwok Pui-lan (Eds.) (2002), *Postcolonialism, Feminism, and Religious Discourse.* New York: Routledge, pp. 62-81.

individual rights, the existence of minority cultural communities within these states complicates the protection and interpretation of these rights.

A Brief Examination of the Group Rights Literature in Political Theory

Political theorists who have sought to delineate the relationship between minority and majority cultures have discussed the individual's relationship to the group, but they have not taken gender into account sufficiently. The right to culture can be said to be merely an individual's right to his or her *own* culture, but several theorists have sought to examine the *collective* nature of the right, because the idea of culture presumes a community in which to participate. The relationship between the individual and the community is also part of a larger debate about the interaction between communities, particularly minority cultures and the multicultural democratic state.

Although this is a large and growing field, examined here are a few scholars representing some of the key positions which are relevant to a further discussion of the relationship between gender and culture. Among the leading scholars in this field, Will Kymlicka is often hailed as a defender of group rights within liberalism. In *Multicultural Citizenship*, Will Kymlicka defines "societal culture," which encompasses "the full range of human activities, including social, educational, religious, recreational, and economic life" for a given people.[12] While Kymlicka shows the varied experiences that define a culture, he does not state that a societal culture necessarily has a "shared language" and "territory."[13] Kymlicka's interest in societal cultures is in the relationship between the majority and minority cultures in Western states, because these groups "are seeking greater recognition and accommodation of their cultural differences" in the multicultural West and "may even seek to secede, if they think their aspirations cannot be met within the existing state."[14] Conflicts between cultural groups and larger societies are not new phenomena nor are conflicts between the majority and the minority within a society. Kymlicka's work addresses these issues in the contemporary period at a time when Western states are increasingly multicultural, and cultural communities

---

[12] Will Kymlicka (1995). *Multicultural Citizenship: A Liberal Theory of Minority Rights*. New York: Oxford University Press, p. 76.

[13] Ibid.

[14] Will Kymlicka (Ed.) (1995). *The Rights of Minority Cultures*. New York: Oxford University Press, p. 3.

can invoke rights-based claims to support their difference from the majority of society.

Traditionally in political theory, the rights of groups have been addressed in the larger liberalism-versus-communitarianism debate, but Kymlicka's work examines the problem of group rights within liberalism itself. Integration of various groups in Western states has been based upon a model of immigration, but Kymlicka is interested in the rights of long-standing national minorities who wish to maintain their cultural distinctiveness,[15] which pose "a deep challenge to all Western political traditions."[16] He argues that a liberal conception of justice requires recognition of some forms of group differentiated rights in order to ensure equality.[17] Differentiated citizenship ensures the minority a voice in the larger society, as well as allowing for limited autonomy,[18] but Kymlicka does not address gender in his examination of group rights. He recognizes that the rights of the group can be distinct from the sum of the rights of its members, but the rights of women are seemingly absent from his conception of multicultural citizenship.

Kymlicka contends that group rights and individual rights can coexist. Chandran Kukathas, one of Kymlicka's best-known critics, however, asserts that liberalism does not require reinterpretation in order to take into account the concerns of groups. Kukathas rejects "the proposition that fundamental moral claims are to be attached to such groups" primarily because of the ever-changing composition and relative social meaning of groups in society.[19] Groups are best seen as associations of individuals in Kukathas's view; and, therefore, the will or character of the group is unknowable, because just as the group may seem to be a dissenting minority within the majority culture, there would also be dissent within the

---

[15] Supra n12, p. 63. Kymlicka agrees with Glazer and Walzer's distinction between immigrants and national minorities because immigration is usually voluntary.

[16] Ibid., p. 74.

[17] Ibid., p. 125.

[18] Other scholars in this debate (e.g., Jeff Spinner-Halev) argue for inclusive multiculturalism in which there are two levels of citizenship. Groups must abide by the formal requirements of citizenship, but can live in isolated communities without state support. However, to enter mainstream society, there will have to be modification of the group in order to adhere to both levels of citizenship. See Jeff Spinner-Halev (1999). "Cultural Pluralism and Partial Citizenship." In Christian Joppke and Steven Lukes (Eds). *Multicultural Questions.* Oxford: Oxford University Press, pp. 81-82.

[19] Chandran Kukathas (1992). "Are There Any Cultural Rights?" *Political Theory,* 20(1): 110.

group.[20] The possibility of a tyrannical majority within a minority culture is incompatible with liberalism.

Kukathas does not suggest that group membership be banned or that the majority culture force illiberal groups to conform to liberal ideals. He recognizes the fact that societies are made up of individuals who have different community memberships that are fundamental to identity, and that individuals may belong to groups that hold illiberal tenets.[21] He contends that the multicultural liberal state can both protect individual rights and respect the existence of illiberal groups if freedom of association is the preeminent societal value, and if individuals are allowed a substantive right to exit a group.[22] The existence of a right of exit would not only give individuals the option to leave groups that impose limits on rights, but it would also create an incentive for internal change among illiberal groups in order to retain members. For Kukathas, the right of exit is the safety valve for the relationship between the majority and minority culture. This focus, though, on the right of exit shows both Kukathas's commitment to the rights of individuals and an underestimation of the extent to which individuals are tied to their cultures. He fails to take into account the influence of religion and culture on individuals, as well as the degree to which gender identity figures into the debate.

In addition, there has been work in political theory which does engage in the group rights dialogue while seeking to broaden the scope of past debates. Bhikhu Parekh's work, for example, attempts to address the question of the multicultural state in a more complex manner that examines the issues of gender and immigration as well as the relationship between the majority and traditional cultural minorities. Parekh separates respecting the existence of other cultures from the equal respect for other cultures: "Respect for a culture therefore means respect for a community's right to its culture and for the content and character of that culture."[23]

While he sets out the parameters of respect, Parekh does not suggest that all groups should be respected, because this respect should, in his view, be contingent upon the evaluation of the principles central to the

---

[20] Kukathas, supra n19, p. 114.

[21] Ibid., pp. 126-127.

[22] Ibid., p. 128. The right to exit has to be "substantive." Kukathas notes (p. 124) that exit is only a viable option when there is "a wider society that is open to individuals wishing to leave their local groups." Without an alternative society, the choice to exit would be purely abstract because "the individual would have to choose between the conformity of the village and the lawlessness (and loneliness) of the heath."

[23] Bhikhu Parekh (2000). *Rethinking Multiculturalism: Cultural Diversity and Political Theory*. Cambridge, MA: Harvard University Press, p. 176.

group's way of life.[24] He suggests the necessity of an "intercultural dia-logue" in which the minority community can appoint a spokesperson to explain a cultural practice which has become a point of contention between the majority and the minority cultures.[25] The spokesperson could explain the importance of the practice and attempt to persuade the majority of the practice's legitimacy. However, if the spokesperson is unsuccessful, the minority should yield to the majority.[26]

While Parekh tries to empower minorities so that they can protect their own cultures through the spokesperson, he contends that the minority should halt its cultural tradition if the majority is unconvinced. The neces-sity of persuasion in his theory shows that the power remains solely with the majority culture. Parekh envisioned a level cultural playing field in which cultures meet for "an open and equal dialogue" in the interest of fairness.[27] However, if individuals have the right to participate in their cultural communities, it would seem a violation of human rights for the access to one's cultural rights to be dependent upon the approval of those outside of the group.

All three scholars seek to protect the rights of individuals while recog-nizing the existence of seemingly illiberal groups in the multicultural state. While Parekh addresses the existence of gender within this debate, his answers are limited because the "intercultural dialogue" is skewed toward the majority. Kukathas's emphasis on exit likewise does not recognize culture as integral to identity nor does Kymlicka's differentiated citizen-ship take into account the problem of the minority within the minority. None of these leading authors examines the complexity that gender adds to the group rights debate.

---

[24] Ibid.

[25] Parekh establishes six conditions for cultural rights claims such as preserving a traditional social order, maintaining community existence, and community recovery from systematic oppression. Ibid., pp. 217-218.

[26] Ibid., pp. 272-273. Monique Deveaux's conception of deliberative liberalism in *Cultural Pluralism and Dilemmas of Justice* is similar to Parekh's multicultural dialogue, but gives more autonomy to the minority community. She recognizes that groups may not be able to articulate claims in ways that are compatible with the dominant legal system, and she also wants to encourage internal criticism of practices. See Monique Deveaux (2000), *Cultural Pluralism and Dilemmas of Justice*. Ithaca, New York: Cornell University Press; Monique Deveaux (2006), *Gender and Justice in the Multicultural State*. Oxford; New York: Oxford University Press.

[27] Supra n23, p. 13.

Western Feminist Scholarship

Western feminist thought has of course addressed gender inequality in the Western world. While scholars have taken various theoretical and political approaches to this issue, there has been a preoccupation in the literature with an individualistic conception of equality. Additionally, the ways in which culture complicates discussions of feminism has not been acknowledged, as I will show. Early Anglo-American feminist thought is a reaction to the exclusion of women from Western political thought. Enlightenment thinkers such as Rousseau espoused the ideal of natural rights and equality, but these were not available to women. Eighteenth century feminists such as Mary Wollstonecraft criticized Rousseau for failing to imagine women as full citizens of society not bound to the home and family: they asserted women's equality.[28] The emphasis of the feminist scholarship of this period is the political inclusion of women as individual citizens in a democratic society, instead of inhabitants of the private sphere alone, in which they are ruled over by men who are the actual citizens and who have dominion in the home over women as well.

The assumed universal nature of women's experience in society is at the heart of feminism throughout its second wave. Betty Friedan's *The Feminine Mystique* and Simone de Beauvoir's *The Second Sex* discuss the problems women face in society. Friedan calls it "the problem that has no name," the feeling women had that they were missing out on something in life, that their roles as wives and mothers were restrictive.[29] Simone de Beauvoir seeks to identify the (often subtle) ways women are treated as "other" than men. The term "human" is defined in male terms: everything from the expected mode of dress to the expected social characteristics of women is socially constructed to make them distinct from men, as merely objects of male desire. While these works both purport to speak for all women, they really only speak for the actual experiences of a few. Their "universalism," as critics such as bell hooks have pointed out, is not only confined to Western culture, but more specifically to a white, middle-class, existence, which is essentialized into a monolithic category of "woman," from which to critique all patriarchal societies.

Radical feminist scholars such as Andrea Dworkin and Catharine MacKinnon focus on violence against women as the single most important

---

[28] Mary Wollstonecraft (1992). *A Vindication of the Rights of Woman*. 1792. New York: Knopf. While women were not explicitly excluded from all Enlightenment thought, Carole Pateman has asserted that patriarchy is a distinctive feature of and implicit in the social contract. See Carole Pateman (1988). *The Sexual Contract*. Stanford, CA: Stanford University Press.

[29] Betty Friedan (1984). *The Feminine Mystique*. 1961. New York: Laurel Books.

manifestation of society's patriarchal structure. They continue to use the category "woman." MacKinnon's work has more often focused on the ways in which the law itself is male and creates a space in which violence against women is never clearly recognized as a legitimate social and political problem. Andrea Dworkin's work challenges women to actively work against a culture of violence against women.[30] She writes in a narrative style that focuses mainly on women's experiences in the Western world. As mentioned earlier in the discussion of FGM, she mentions culture only in a negative context. In her view, all societies are organized to be detrimental to the rights of women.

Western feminist scholars have long asserted the existence of a patriarchal superstructure in which world cultures are formed that would explain the seemingly universal existence of male-dominated societies. Although Western feminist scholarship has moved in new directions, this worldview of the earlier radical feminists has shaped the women's human rights literature that I will discuss.

The insistence upon a purely individualistic conception of rights in these feminist texts leaves out group dynamics. Because the conflict between majority and minority cultures is already present, feminist thought that does not acknowledge culture creates a situation in which women's rights become a battle ground between societies. Liberating women from patriarchal culture can be construed as cultural imperialism.[31]

Women's Relationship to Culture: A Brief Literature Review

Several scholars have sought to examine the relationship between feminism and multiculturalism, but Susan Moller Okin provides the most well-known link between feminist political thought and multiculturalism. In her 1999 work *Is Multiculturalism Bad for Women?*, Susan Moller Okin reacted against the growing literature in the field of multiculturalism and

---

[30] See Andrea Dworkin (1987), *Intercourse*, New York: The Free Press; and Andrea Dworkin (1997), *Life and Death*, New York: The Free Press.

[31] Third World and Postcolonial Feminists have resisted the entire notion of culture that theorists like Kymlica put forth because it of the idea that culture permeates all aspects of a society and that culture is seen as uniform among a group. Selya Benhabib, for example, rejects Kymlicka's idea of societal culture because she does not believe there can be a unified culture whose members all share certain traits. "Cultures are not homogeneous wholes; they are self-definitions and symbolizations which their members articulate in the course of partaking of complex social and significative practices." Selya Benhabib (1999). "'Nous' et 'les Autres': The Politics of Complex Cultural Dialogue in a Global Civilization." In Christian Joppke and Steven Lukes (Eds.). *Multicultural Questions*. Oxford: Oxford University Press, pp. 53-54.

cultural rights, suggesting that the emphasis on culture is detrimental to women because cultures are patriarchal and cultural rights are often invoked against women's rights.[32] Expanding on this point in other work, she has argued that the way in which culture has been defined by those seeking group rights leaves out the concerns of women and sexual minorities, because they are not perceived as having culture and they are usually seen as opposing norms of the group.[33]

Okin, a prominent political theorist and feminist scholar, includes in her article short examples of what she felt was cultural toleration, which had created a rights-based form of gender oppression. Her arguments are persuasive but rest on several assumptions. She briefly cites cases to illustrate the problem minority cultures pose for the protection of women's rights, but the discussion is too simplistic. Without teasing out the details of the complex relationship between women and their communities, generalizations cannot be made that show that women's lives are necessarily at risk from their communities. Okin makes this point clear in "Feminism and Multiculturalism: Some Tensions" where she asserts that "[i]n the case of a more patriarchal minority culture in the context of a less patriarchal majority culture, no argument can be made on the basis of the enhancement of self-respect or the greater capacity for choice that female members of the culture have any clear interest in its preservation."[34] Her challenge to feminists to strive against oppression in the private sphere and not to allow culture as a defense against the violation of women's rights[35] relies on two assumptions: 1) culture is patriarchal, and 2) gender rights are only available to individuals. Implicit in Okin's characterization of the debate between gender and cultural rights is the perspective that group rights limit the rights of the individual in all circumstances.

Okin's work has drawn both praise and criticism, but the question she poses is at the heart of the debate over gender and cultural rights. She criticizes the right of exit that scholars such as Kymlicka use to support the toleration of illiberal groups within liberal society because she contends that gender changes the substance of the exit option. Women, she contends, may not wish to leave or may not be able to do so, due to oppression. She stresses that women should not have to leave; they should be able

---

[32] Susan Moller Okin (1999). *Is Multiculturalism Bad for Women?* Princeton: Princeton University Press.

[33] Susan Moller Okin (1998). "Feminism and Multiculturalism: Some Tensions." *Ethics*, 108(4): 662.

[34] Supra n23, p. 680.

[35] See also Susan Moller Okin (1998). "Feminism, Women's Human Rights, and Cultural Differences." *Hypatia*, 13(2): 32-52.

to demand equality within the group.[36] As I stated earlier, other Western feminist theorists such as Andrea Dworkin and Mary Daly have sought to show the universal oppression and violence women face from their own societies. However, the question in the title of her article echoes the concerns of Parekh that unchecked multiculturalism will create a human rights void in which all practices are acceptable even if they violate the rights of individuals.

Some critics, like Leti Volpp, contend that Okin's focus on female circumcision, the headscarf debate in France, and dowry death oversimplify culture and portray non-Western women as perpetual victims of culture who can only be rescued by Western feminists.[37] Volpp contends that a focus on "cultural violence" skews the debate and obscures other social forces in women's lives.[38] While Western culture recognizes its history and progress, non-Western cultures are seen as static and ahistorical because "[t]hose with power appear to have no culture; those without power are culturally endowed."[39] The focus on the so-called negative aspects of non-Western and minority cultures predetermines the conclusions from such an endeavor—(minority) culture is inherently harmful. Volpp rightly questions the strict binary that theorists such as Okin draw between feminism and multiculturalism. Her comparisons between U.S. and non-Western policies affecting women illustrate the universality of the patriarchy, but her analysis ends there. She offers excellent questions for future debate, but, in the end, hopes for an open dialogue about the full meaning of "women's rights as human rights" and offers no clear solutions.

Ayelet Shachar seeks to clarify the relationship between minority cultures and the multicultural state in regards to the rights of women. Her work focuses on respecting the rights of the group while protecting its members. Shachar argues that family is the basis for determining group membership. However, granting a group exclusive authority in this legal arena is problematic for women because of the potential for discrimination.[40] She challenges Kymlicka's "all-too-easy distinction between 'exter-

---

[36] Susan Moller Okin (2002). "'Mistresses of Their Own Destiny': Group Rights, Gender and Realistic Rights of Exit." *Ethics*, 112(2): 205-230.

[37] Leti Volpp (2002). "Feminism v. Multiculturalism." *Columbia Law Review* 101: 1183.

[38] Ibid., p. 1208.

[39] Ibid., p. 1192.

[40] Ayelet Shachar (1999). "The Paradox of Multicultural Vulnerability." In Christian Joppke and Steven Lukes (Eds.). *Multicultural Questions*. Oxford: Oxford University Press, pp. 99-100.

nal' and 'internal' aspects of accommodation"[41] and proposes instead a more nuanced notion of "transformative accommodation" in which the state and the group share jurisdiction over the group members' lives.[42] Neither the culture nor the state would have complete control over an individual, meaning that compromise and dialogue would be crucial. Shachar's framework is based upon her application of theory to several examples in which women face a choice between discrimination within their cultural group or complete separation from it.

Shachar's conception of transformative jurisdiction[43] does not fully address the relationship between gender and culture. The resolution of women's rights' limbo becomes a sharing of jurisdiction over matters affecting women's individual rights. Implicit in her discussion of rights is the conception of marriage and family as the only area of law in which gender and cultural rights conflicts occur. Also implicit is an individualistic conception of culture. While Ayelet Shachar presents several detailed examples to underscore her points, her examples, like those of Susan Okin, all demonstrate a cultural group's denial of individual rights based upon gender, but the idea of women's culture within a minority culture is absent.

In a similar vein to Ayelet Shachar, Sarah Song examines the relationship between gender and culture. Her work argues for rights-respecting accommodationism as a way to balance gender and culture in multicultural liberal societies.[44] Song recognizes women's commitment to their cultural identities, yet also is concerned that culture has the capacity to be harmful to women. Her work seeks to show the complexity of culture as well as the complexity of societies' responses, which contain within them assumptions about the minority culture and gender. Although her work makes use of cases to give a more in-depth analysis, , the cases mostly seem to show the ways in which culture is problematic for women and from which they therefore may be in need of protection. This scholarship, like that of Shachar, represents an important step in investigating the relationship

---

[41] Ayelet Shachar (2001). *Multicultural Jurisdictions: Cultural Differences and Women's Rights*. Cambridge, UK: Cambridge University Press, p. 12.

[42] Ibid., p. 126.

[43] Kymlicka disagrees with Shachar's notion of shared authority because he suspects that state intervention may not appeal to all minority groups. He contends that people are simultaneously members of multiple political communities and that the nation-state may not be the political entity with which a group would be willing to share authority, due to discriminatory past dealings with the state. Will Kymlicka (1999). "Comments on Shachar and Spinner-Halev: An Update from the Multiculturalism Wars." In Christian Joppke and Steven Lukes (Eds.). *Multicultural Questions*. Oxford: Oxford University Press, pp. 117-119.

[44] Sarah Song (2007). *Justice, Gender, and the Politics of Multiculturalism*. New York: Cambridge University Press, p. 8.

between gender and culture, but it does not fully explore the interaction between these rights because of the seemingly underlying emphasis on the possible harm to women. In contrast, my work will attempt to further complexify the relationship between gender and culture and will argue for an approach to cultural rights that fully takes the interaction between gender and culture into account.

Stepping outside of work focused on gender and multiculturalism, Critical Race Feminism's examination of the intersection of gender and race offers important insight to the discussion of gender and culture. Paulette Caldwell contends that "[r]acism and sexism are interlocking, mutually reinforcing components of a system of dominance rooted in patriarchy."[45] Kimberlé Crenshaw looks at particular types of women's rights claims—rape and domestic violence—to argue that African American women face particular hardships in these areas because their experiences fall at the intersection of race and gender. She contends that the feminist agenda on the issues of domestic violence and rape has been constructed around the concerns of white women, and "the narratives of race are based on the experience of black men."[46] Where Crenshaw shows how both gender and race work together to obscure the experiences and identities of women of color on issues of violence against women, Paulette Caldwell examines the more subtle interaction between gender and race that bars women of color from rights claims that arise out of cultural difference. In her essay "A Hair Piece," she discusses the legal barriers African American women face in challenging dress codes that disallow braids. Because these hairstyles are particular to specific in both gender and race, African American women cannot claim to be victims of purely racial or gender discrimination. American law does not recognize the existence of a category of African American women. Similarly, a conception of women's culture within a community is absent from the literature. Women have had to choose between their gender and their culture. The law protects either, but not both.

While Caldwell examined gender and race in American law, the same legal void is evident in international human rights. Women are situated in their cultural communities and make decisions reflecting both individual desires and community and cultural values. Because gender and culture

---

45 Paulette M. Caldwell. "A Hair Piece: Perspectives on the Intersection of Race and Gender." In Adrien Katherine Wing (Ed.) (1997). *Critical Race Feminism: A Reader*. New York: New York University Press. p. 301.

46 Kimberlé Williams Crenshaw. "Mapping the Margins: Intersectionality, Identity Politics, and Violence against Women of Color." In Kimberlé Williams Crenshaw, et al. (Eds.). *The Key Writings that Formed the Movement*. New York: The New Press, p. 376.

are integral to identity, "opting out" is not an appropriate solution. Crenshaw points out that the intersection of these two can even create a unique space in which an individual's rights are served by neither gender nor race [or culture] alone. I want to extend this reasoning further to suggest that the choice between gender and culture ignores the existence of women's culture within a community. Western gender theory and the group rights literature do not address a notion of women's culture, and the international human rights discourse has not addressed this problem either.

Cultural Rights under International Law

Although minority rights provisions are absent from the *Universal Declaration of Human Rights,* the ICCPR and the ICESCR do make reference to the protection of minorities and cultural rights. The ICESCR states in Article 15 that everyone has the right "to take part in cultural life." *The International Covenant on Civil Political Rights* offers a stronger statement in Article 27:

> In those states in which ethnic, religious, or linguistic minorities exist, persons belonging to such minorities shall not be denied the right, in community with other members of their group, to enjoy their own culture, to profess and practise their own religion, or to use their own language.[47]

The right to be part of one's cultural community is specifically mentioned for persons belonging to a minority group. However, as Jeremy Waldron points out, Article 27 grants these collective rights without a clear definition of the terms.[48] United Nations Special Rapporteur Francesco Capotorti sought to provide a clear definition in his 1977 report for the UN. He wrote that minority rights applied to individuals who were members of a minority population of a state whose members share "ethnic, religious or linguistic characteristics differing from those of the rest of the population and show, if only implicitly, a sense of solidarity, directed towards preserving their culture, traditions, religion or language."[49] Individual members

---

[47] United Nations (1966). *International Covenant on Civil and Political Rights*, Article 27.

[48] Jeremy Waldron (1995). "Minority Cultures and the Cosmopolitan Alternative." In Will Kymlicka (Ed.) (1995). *The Rights of Minority Cultures* (supra n11), p. 97. However, the Human Rights Committee has sought to clarify Article 27 in General Comment 23. Human Rights Committee (1994). *General Comment No. 23: The Rights of Minorities (Art. 27): 08/04/94.* Geneva, Switzerland: United Nations. CCPR/C21/Rev.1/Add.5. Manfred Nowak also provides commentary on the articles of the ICCPR. See Manfred Nowak (1993). *UN Convention on Civil and Political Rights: CCPR Commentary.* Arlington, VA: N.P. Engel.

[49] Francesco Capotorti (1991). *Study on the Rights of Persons Belonging to Ethnic, Religious and Linguistic Minorities.* New York: United Nations.

can be beneficiaries of rights that protect the group, but the group itself has no legal personality. Patrick Thornberry, on the other hand, writes that the rights enumerated in Article 27 are a hybrid of individual and collective rights, and that international law is inconsistent on the topic of minority rights.[50] Groups cannot access their human rights because the laws have been created with a bias towards individuals.

While the emphasis in human rights documents has been placed on individual rights, there are provisions that protect group rights as well. Group rights are inherently those rights that only can be exercised and enjoyed by a collective. Examples of such rights are the right to culture and the right to self-determination. Because legal systems, including the Human Rights Committee in the United Nations, are set up to protect and recognize mainly individual rights, the legal systems cannot "fully address the concerns of those intent on preserving the integrity of their groups."[51] Adjudicating group claims on the international level is difficult because "states themselves are the dominant players within the international law system."[52] The state requires a group to prove its claims, which can be at times antithetical to that group's own customary laws and traditional beliefs. The focus on individual rights in the international human rights instruments illustrates the assumption that the protection of groups is accomplished through the protection of the rights of the individual members.[53] What this premise fails to account for is that the rights groups

---

[50] Patrick Thornberry (1991). *International Law and the Rights of Minorities*. Oxford: Clarendon Press. See also Athanasia Spiliopoulou Akermark (1997). *Justifications of Minority Protection in International Law*. London; Boston: Kluwer Law International. Akermark separates minority rights from the protection of the minority. Protection includes prevention of discrimination and correction of past discrimination, but its negative conception allows one to accept the international instruments' minority provisions without debating positive group rights (pp. 50-54). She also notes that the Human Rights Committee's interpretation of the ICCPR has demonstrated a commitment to culture as well as individual rights (p. 179). See also Elsa Stamatopolou (2007). *Cultural Rights and International Law: Article 27 of the UDHR and Beyond*. Leiden: Martinus Nijhoff Publishers.

[51] Richard Herz (1993). "Legal Protection for Indigenous Cultures: Sacred Sites and Communal Rights." *Virginia Law Review*, 79(3): 697.

[52] Ibid., p. 694.

[53] Ian Brownlie (1992). *Treaties and Indigenous Peoples*. Oxford: Clarendon Press; New York: Oxford University Press, 36. See also the Kukathas/Kymlicka debate. Chandran Kukathas (1992), "Are There Any Cultural Rights?" *Political Theory*, 20(1): 105-139; and Will Kymlicka (1995), *Multicultural Citizenship: A Liberal Theory of Minority Rights*. Oxford: Clarendon Press. Kukathas argues that right to association should be the framework in which cultural rights are discussed and that the right to culture is not a separate right. Kukathas argues against group rights, while Kymlicka supports them.

retain cannot be protected through allowing their protection on an individual level. The right to culture is a right for the enjoyment of a *group*.

The Literature on Women's Human Rights

The women's human rights literature runs parallel to feminist theory scholarship, but focuses on promoting women's human rights through international instruments such as the Women's Convention. Just as Western feminists criticize the ways women have been left out of political thought, international law scholars argue for the need for separate human rights instruments to protect women because of the distinct issues women face in invoking their rights.[54] *The Convention on the Elimination of All Forms of Discrimination against Women* codifies women's human rights and reflects the Western feminist thought of the 1970s and the women's human rights scholarship. Charlotte Bunch explores the meaning of women's human rights and contends that there is a need to focus on violence against women as a serious problem affecting women around the globe. She states that it is necessary to discuss "women's human rights" as opposed to simply discussing human rights, because in the human rights discourse and in the struggle against human rights abuses, "female victims are often invisible, because the dominant image of the political actor in our world is male."[55] As the term "human rights" implies, these are inherent rights that both men and women should enjoy upon the basis of their existence. Bunch points out that the patriarchally structured world has given way to a construction of human rights in which only men can enjoy them and only a man can be recognized as the victim when these rights are violated.

The universalist stance Bunch and others take is open to similar criticisms that second-wave feminists faced. Their project seeks to unite all women, but, as scholars such as Vasuki Nesiah contend, it leaves out the voices of women in the developing world because the international character of women's rights is built upon a presumably universal experience of

---

[54] For further discussion of women's human rights in international law, see Rebecca J. Cook (Ed.) (1994), *Human Rights of Women: National and International Perspectives*, Philadelphia: University of Pennsylvania Press; and Julie Peters and Andrea Wolper (Eds.) (1995), *Women's Rights/Human Rights: International Feminist Perspectives*, New York: Routledge.

[55] Charlotte Bunch (1990). "Women's Rights as Human Rights: Toward a Re-Vision of Human Rights." *Human Rights Quarterly*, 12(4): 486. See also Rebecca J. Cook (Ed.) (1994). *Human Rights of Women: National and International Perspectives*. Philadelphia: University of Pennsylvania Press.

oppression.[56] Given the emphasis on shared experience and the presumption of patriarchy in all cultures, women's human rights in both the Women's Convention and in scholarship reflect the perceived tensions between gender and cultural rights. Proponents of cultural relativism contend the scholarship and the convention impose a monolithic view of gender rights and reflect Western cultural values.

To combat this contention, scholars such as Eva Brems examine the problem facing theorists of synthesizing the seemingly opposing concepts of human rights for women and respecting the right to culture. She argues that feminists and proponents of cultural relativism share common ground, especially in their respective critiques of human rights and the Enlightenment discourse of law and rights. However, her suggestion that these opposing theorists collaborate in order to "develop a powerful constructive human rights critique" does not solve the central, underlying concern regarding the development of a cross-cultural women's human rights perspective.[57] In fact, although Brems argues for a notion of inclusive universality in which the core of a human right should be maintained, she also allows for flexibility and transformation within societies. Therefore, her work is focused on individual rights and does not adequately address the cultural component.[58]

The notion of flexibility is central to the work of other women's human rights scholars. Oloka-Onyango and Tamale's article, "'The Personal is Political,' or Why Women's Rights are Indeed Human Rights," criticizes the cultural relativist argument that often challenges women's rights and upholds the right to culture over universalist definitions of rights. They suggest that positing women's human rights within the human rights

---

[56] Nesiah goes on to point out that this shared feminist agenda based on experience preferences the concerns of "first world" scholars and makes women in the developing world into powerless victims of oppression. Vasuki Nesiah (1993). "Toward a Feminist Internationality: A Critique of US Legal Scholarship." In Adrien Katherine Wing (Ed.) (2000). *Global Critical Race Feminism: An International Reader*. New York: New York University Press, pp. 43 and 48.

[57] Eva Brems (1997). "Enemies or Allies? Feminism and Cultural Relativism as Dissident Voices in Human Rights Discourse." *Human Rights Quarterly* 19: 164.

[58] Eva Brems (2001). *Human Rights: Universality and Diversity*. The Hague; Boston: Kluwer Law International. She contends that some traditions are "harmful cultural practices" (such as a conservative interpretation of shari'a) are incompatible with human rights. Her solution, in order to guard against claims of imperialism, is to support opponents of these traditions within societies.

framework allows "adequate space for a diversity of perspectives."[59] They contend that using the popular slogan "the personal is political" allows for that diversity of problems across cultures and provides space within the framework of human rights to address the concerns of all women. However, even the diversity of interpretation of women's human rights is predicated upon individual rights found in the scholarship and international instruments.

Women and Human Rights Law

Like its philosophical predecessors, such as *The Declaration of the Rights of Man*, the UDHR sought to enumerate the basic rights we should all share within a society simply on the basis of our existence as humans. The term "everyone" is used instead of "men" or "all men" in order to make the document, and human rights in general, gender neutral. This interest in neutrality, though, implicitly excludes women because nothing in the document specifically addresses the ways in which women's human rights are violated.

Evidence of this exclusion is found in Articles 23 and 25, which deal with wages and standard of living. Article 23.3 states that "[e]veryone who works has the right to just and favorable remuneration insuring *himself and his family* an existence worthy of human dignity, and supplemented, if necessary, by other means of social protection." Article 25.1 states "[e]veryone has the right to a standard of living adequate for the health and well-being of *himself and of his family*[.]"[60] Both of these statements define "everyone" as the collective pronoun for all men within society. The family, which would include women and children, is defined as an appendage to or the property of a man. He has the right to work and earn wages; he is the human. This passage posits women as beings existing only within the family unit and accepts the division of labor between the sexes as natural. This endorsement of the labor division maintains the public/private spheres that exist within society in which the realm of citizenship, rights, and laws exist in the public sphere traditionally inhabited by men. Women, because they are traditionally confined to the home (which law and society

---

59 J. Oloka-Onyango and Sylvia Tamale (1995). "'The Personal is Political,' or Why Women's Rights are Indeed Human Rights: An African Perspective on International Feminism." *Human Rights Quarterly*, 3(2): 713.

60 United Nations General Assembly (1948). *The Universal Declaration of Human Rights* in Ian Brownlie (Ed.) (1995). *Basic Documents of in International Law*, 4th ed. Oxford: Clarendon Press.

typically do not invade), inhabit the private sphere.[61] As feminist scholars contend, international human rights law is predicated on the distinction between public and private spheres. Women's concerns are relegated to the private sphere, but human rights claims center on the public sphere.[62] Although many delegates to the Drafting Committee sought to create a gender-neutral document, the women's lobby allowed these articles to stand without removal of the sexist language.[63] The UDHR does not only enumerate political and civil rights that would make its Articles only applicable to the public sphere of life, however. It addresses economic, social, and cultural rights as well, such as marriage and language, but these rights still do not address the specific situation of women. Because women are not specifically included, they are essentially excluded not only from this document, but also human rights discourse in general.

Major human rights instruments that followed maintained this implicit exclusion of women. Women and men were supposedly equal with regard to their human rights under international law.[64] However, even a cursory analysis of wording in the UDHR and human rights treaties calls into question this commitment to equality. More importantly, the implementation of human rights instruments has left women unable to invoke their fundamental human rights. This is because they ignore the specific ways in which women's human rights are violated and make these treaties in effect "not apply to these obvious violations of the human rights of women."[65]

Women's human rights have been considered since the UN's inception. The Economic and Social Council, better known as ECOSOC created the Commission on Human Rights and the Sub-Commission on the Status of Women in 1946. The Sub-Commission was upgraded to the Commission on the Status of Women (CSW) in 1947.[66] From the beginning, issues of human rights differed from those of women. This separation of the concerns of women from human rights is evident in the UDHR. The treatment and development of the CSW underscores the seemingly lesser importance of women's human rights within the United Nations and international law.

---

[61] For a discussion on the public/private divide, see Carole Pateman (1988). *The Sexual Contract*. Stanford, CA: Stanford University Press.

[62] Hilary Charlesworth et al. "Feminist Approaches to International Law." *American Journal of International Law*, 85(4): 629.

[63] Johannes Morsink (1991). "Women's Rights in the Universal Declaration." *Human Rights Quarterly*. 13(2): 242.

[64] See Laura Reanda (1981). "Human Rights and Women's Rights: The United Nations Approach." *Human Rights Quarterly*, 3(2): 13. See also Charlesworth et al., supra n62.

[65] Reanda, supra n64, p. 15.

[66] Ibid., p. 23.

The CSW never met as often as the Commission on Human Rights, has no power to hear individual complaints, and has little investigative power. Eventually in 1966, the CSW prepared the *Draft Declaration on the Elimination of Discrimination against Women* and sent it to the UN General Assembly, but it was not considered until a revised draft was adopted the next year. Attempts to implement this declaration of principles regarding the rights of women led to the creation of the *Convention on the Elimination of All Forms of Discrimination against Women*, better known as the Women's Convention.[67]

The Convention on the Elimination of All Forms of Discrimination Against Women

The most comprehensive list of human rights as they specifically relate to women (often called the Women's Convention) entered into force in CEDAW in 1981.[68] This document serves as both an instrument of international law and "a political manifesto, clearly declaring the right of women to equality and non-discrimination[.]"[69] The four parts of the Convention are intended to "respect, protect, provide, and promote" the human rights of women.[70] Article 1 contains the Convention's definition of discrimination, which states:

> The term 'discrimination against women' shall mean any distinction, exclusion, or restriction made on the basis of sex which has the effect or purpose of impairing or nullifying the recognition, enjoyment or exercise by women, irrespective of their marital status, on the basis of equality of men and women, of human rights and fundamental freedoms in the political, economic, social, cultural, civil or any other field.[71]

There are a few key features in this definition. First, the Convention's purpose as stated in this article is to address "'discrimination against women.'"[72] Second, "[t]he article refers to *effect* as well as *purpose*, thus directing attention to the consequences of governmental measures as well

---

[67] Ibid., p. 21.

[68] *The Convention on the Elimination of All Forms of Discrimination against Women*. Available at www.un.org./Depts/Treaty.

[69] Andrew Byrnes (1998). "The Convention on the Elimination of All Forms of Discrimination Against Women" (unpublished paper, on file with author), p 3.

[70] Philip Alston and Henry J. Steiner (Eds.) (1996). *International Human Rights in Context: Law, Politics, Morals*. Oxford: Clarendon Press, p. 907.

[71] United Nations General Assembly (1979). *The Convention on the Elimination of All Forms of Discrimination against Women*, Article 1.

[72] Supra n70, p. 907.

as the intentions underlying them."[73] The convention allows states to not simply make women equal through laws and policies that assume them to be the same as men, but to enact laws and policies that are female-specific, which allow women to access and enjoy their equal rights with men. Third, this aspect of the definition allows the treaty to apply not only to the government, but also to the society as a whole; therefore, under this convention the government is responsible for creating a society in which equality can exist.[74] While past human rights treaties, such as the ICCPR and the ICESCR, *separated* civil and political rights from economic, social, and cultural rights, the Women's Convention sought to *synthesize* them because women's human rights are affected in all of these aspects of social life. This convention integrates these different types of rights in order to enable women full access to all human rights.[75]

The convention's thirty articles describe discrimination against women, instruct member-states on how to create equality and end discrimination, and also create the Committee on the Elimination of Discrimination against Women (CEDAW). CEDAW is composed of 23 members chosen from states party to the convention and are supposed to represent diverse fields, legal systems, and geographic regions.[76] It collects and reviews reports from member-states regarding their implementation of the convention, as well as issuing recommendations regarding the convention's interpretation.[77] The Women's Convention is the only UN treaty designed solely to protect the rights of women. It integrates the different types of rights into a comprehensive document intended to apply to all women throughout the world.

Limitations of the Women's Convention

The controversial nature of the convention is easily apparent when one examines the reservations states parties have entered. More than thirty states have entered reservations to the convention whereas there has been only a handful to the other conventions such as the *Convention Against*

---

73 Ibid., p. 907.

74 Supra n70.

75 Supra n69.

76 Supra n71, Article 17.

77 Unlike the Human Rights Committee created by the ICCPR and the Economic, Social, and Cultural Committee created by the ICESCR, CEDAW does not currently have the power to hear cases regarding discrimination against women in member-states. The treaty itself contains no individual complaint mechanism. An Optional Protocol to this convention is currently circulating among states. When it enters into force, it will create a mechanism for hearing complaints similar to that of the Human Rights Committee.

Racial Discrimination (CRD). Many countries such as Bangladesh refuse to be bound by provisions interpreted as conflicting with the Islamic law or Shari' a. For example, Bangladesh, Iraq, and other states refused to be bound by parts of Article 2 which outlines the ways in which a state should seek to end discrimination against women and Article 16 that sets forth the ways in which states should enact laws and policies to make men and women equal within the home and family.[78] The sheer number of reservations alone shows the unwillingness of states to fully support the international legal effort at creating equality for women.

As illustrated by the reservations cited above, many states objected on cultural and religious grounds and contended that enacting several of the Women's Convention's provisions in order to protect the rights of women would, in turn, violate those countries' religious and/or cultural rights as protected in other treaties. This change leaves the convention open to charges of Western, cultural imperialism and renders it ineffective as a "political manifesto" for women around the world.[79] The Women's Convention may be one of the most ratified, but it is also one of the weakest.[80]

The Women's Convention was created with high expectations, but its guiding body, CEDAW, and the convention itself have not been a cure-all for gender rights problems. There is no individual complaints mechanism,[81] and many countries have entered reservations to the Convention. While Andrew Byrnes noted that only a few states had entered reservations to the *Convention on the Elimination of All Forms of Racial Discrimination*, numerous states had entered "significant reservations" to the Women's Convention and the acceptance of so many reservations has made it seem less official and less binding.[82] For example, several states have objected to Article 2, which defines discrimination against women!

---

[78] See supra n70, pp. 920-921; and supra n71, Articles 2 and 16.

[79] Supra n69, p. 3.

[80] Supra n59, p. 715.

[81] There is an Optional Protocol for the Convention that would allow for individual complaints, but, even though it does allow for individuals and groups to bring actions, the cause of the complaints has to be individual harm. See Emilia Della Torre (2000). "Women's Business: The Development of an Optional Protocol to the United Nations Women's Convention." *Australian Journal of Human Rights* 6(2): 181-193.

[82] Religion, particularly Islam, has been given as a reason for the reservations to the Women's Convention. Brandt and Kaplan suggest that allowing those reservations to stand could undermine the efficacy of the Convention. However, I contend that the Convention's lack of acknowledgement of culture and religion make its acceptance more difficult. Michele Brandt and Jeffrey A. Kaplan (1995). "The Tension between Women's Rights and Religious Rights: Reservations to CEDAW by Egypt, Bangladesh, and Tunisia." *Journal of Law and Religion* 12(1): 105-142.

While the problems with the Women's Convention appear to be in the realm of enforcement, the document itself does not encompass the full range of women's human rights issues and reflects the same individualistic conception of women's rights found in the Western feminist literature.[83] Several articles in the Convention have been controversial because they may conflict with religion and culture. Article 5, especially, has been the focus of much criticism because it provides in paragraph (a) for states to "modify the social and cultural patterns of conduct of men and women, with a view of achieving the elimination of prejudices and customary and all other practices which are based on the idea of the inferiority or the superiority of the sexes or on stereotyped roles for men and women."[84] While the goals of this article are to create a social space in which women may fully access their human rights, the Convention presents gender equality as dependent upon eliminating cultural practices. This reinforces the view that women have to be rescued from culture.

The Women's Convention focuses on individual rights for women, and its seemingly negative view of culture is fortified by other work in the field of women's human rights. For example, Halima Embarek Warzazi, United Nations Special Rapporteur on Traditional Practices Affecting Health of Women and Children, attempts to sidestep the gender and culture debate by condemning only "bad practices" not "bad cultures."[85] Some practices are deemed incongruent with women's human rights, although it is acknowledged that they are part of culture.[86] However, the contention that certain customs should be blocked reflects the conception of mutually exclusive categories of gender and culture.

---

[83] Celina Romany, for example, argues that the Convention is limiting because it contains an essentialist conception of gender. See Celina Romany. "Themes for a Conversation on Race and Gender in International Human Rights Law." In Adrien Katherine Wing (Ed.) (2000). *Global Critical Race Feminism: An International Reader.* New York: New York University Press, pp. 53-66.

[84] Supra n53, Article 5.

[85] See Halima Embarek Warzazi (1999). *Third Report of the Special Rapporteur on Traditional Practices Affecting the Health of Women and the Girl Child.* New York: United Nations. Submitted to Sub-Commission on the Prevention of Discrimination and Protection of Minorities, E/CN.4/Sub.2/1999/14, July 9, 1999. See also supra n9, discussing FGM.

[86] Third World and Postcolonial Feminists like Uma Narayan challenge the depiction of these practices. Narayan questions the notion of these practices as integral to culture by pointing out that the traditions are rooted in both male-dominated society and colonialism. More broadly, she opposes the notion of societal culture because it cannot be separated from politics in her opinion, and obscures the differences among groups of women. See Uma Narayan (1998). "Essence of Culture and a Sense of History: A Feminist Critique of Cultural Essentialism." *Hypatia,* 13(2): 86-106.

Redefining Gender and Culture

While much of the literature focuses on the supposed opposition be-tween gender and cultural rights, some scholars examine the ways in which culture and religion are related to gender, and use religion and culture as a starting point for women's empowerment. Azizah al-Hibri's work, for example, illustrates the ways in which religion can be a location of empow-erment. She contends that Muslim women can advance rights claims through Islamic jurisprudence that reflects a more accurate interpretation of the Qur'an.[87] Other scholars, such as Bahia Tahzib-Lie, examine the connection between gender and religion in order to show that women can find empowerment through religion and argue that women must be given the right to be full participants in their religion and culture.[88] In addition to the ways in which religion can help to frame gender rights claims and empower women, scholars such as Anne Griffiths examine the more fluid relationship between gender and culture. She favors a pluralist view of women's experiences because gender and culture both affect women's choices in varying ways.[89] Her study of marriage disputes in Botswana shows how women sometimes frame their arguments within the cultural discourse, but, while Griffiths shows the importance of culture in regards to marriage in Botswana, she does not advocate a broader conception of the relationship between gender and culture. A more complete under-standing of the interaction between gender and cultural rights is absent from the literature.

Both in human rights theory and in international law, there is a mis-understanding of the relationship between women and culture. Interna-tional law has enshrined the right to culture, but the relationship between group rights and individual rights remains unsolved. The major scholars of group rights do not adequately address the particular situation of women. Feminist theorists and women's human rights scholars do not sufficiently examine the role of culture in women's lives. This gap in the literature is

---

[87] Azizah Y. al-Hibri (1997). "Islam, Law, and Custom: Redefining Muslim Women's Rights." *American University Journal of International Law and Religion,* 12(1): 44. See also Azizah Y. al-Hibri. "Deconstructing Patriarchal Jurisprudence in Islamic Law: A Faithful Approach." In Adrien Katherine Wing (Ed.) (2000). *Global Critical Race Feminism: An International Reader.* New York: New York University Press, pp. 221-233.

[88] Bahia Tahzib-Lie (2000). "Applying a Gender Perspective in the Area of the Right to Freedom of Religion or Belief." *Brigham Young University Law Review,* 2000(3): 967-987.

[89] Griffiths objects to a universal category of "woman" because it does not recognize the broad range of women's experiences. Anne Griffiths (2001). "Gendering Culture: Towards a Plural Perspective on Kwena Women's Rights." In Jane K. Cowan et al. (Eds.) (2001). *Culture and Rights: Anthropological Perspectives.* Cambridge: Cambridge University Press.

reflected in the major human rights conventions. The Women's Convention reflects the feminist thought of the 1970s and incorporates Western feminist thought into its articles. It calls for women's liberation through the abandonment of culture. The lack of recognition of the importance of culture to the lives of women, as well as the limited view of culture, obscures the multilayered identity of women. It puts rights in conflict with one another and forces women to choose one element of their identity over another. It also obscures any notion of women's culture.

Toward a Theory of Gendered Cultural Rights

Women are not victims of culture. Women's human rights do not require the death of culture. For women to have full access to their human rights they must be allowed to reclaim the notion of culture. The multilayered identity of women requires a re-imagining of culture in which women's roles and traditions are seen as cultural contributions that have the potential capacity for empowerment in both the public and private spheres. Instead of a point of division that allows for the characterization of women's human rights as Western, a gendered notion of culture allows women's human rights to be more inclusive.

This notion of gendered cultural rights is of utmost importance in the examination of perceived conflicts between gender and culture in the Western multicultural state. A solely Western-based concept of individual rights seem incompatible to cultural communities with strong group identity. Furthermore, the perception that women's rights can be served only in the individual context blocks women from many human rights claims and forces the unfair choice between culture and gender.

As I explore the meaning of gendered cultural rights, I examine several key "battlegrounds" between women's human rights and culture. The research in this field has traditionally focused on issues of marriage and family; however, this is a limiting way to view women's experiences with their cultural communities. The four case studies I provide demonstrate how gendered cultural rights can work as a framework for understanding a human rights situation in which a rights claim would either not fit within established rights or would not allow for a solution which would allow group members, especially women, to protect both gender and cultural rights.

Although each case demonstrates a different aspect of the complex relationship between gender and culture, neither previous commentators nor the women at the heart of each controversy have clearly defined these cases as human rights issues. Although gendered cultural rights exist worldwide, culture varies around the globe. The cases, therefore, are situated within national contexts because the meaning of even the same cultural tradition can vary, further illustrating the importance of in-depth analysis. Gendered cultural rights frames these cases as human rights concerns, opening up new avenues for making human rights-based claims in international and domestic contexts. In addition to legal claims, this new category of human rights would give women in these cases the opportunity to engage in advocacy and coalition-building with national and transnational human rights non-governmental organizations. Gendered cultural rights can bring new mechanisms through which to address women's concerns and new allies to human rights dilemmas that have in the past been seen as rights conflicts.

Description of Chapters

The case of Sandra Lovelace is a recurring theme. This decision recognized that women have a human right to be part of their cultures, a right that should be protected under international human rights laws and by national governments. However, the meaning of a woman's right to culture has not been examined and included in international human rights law or policy. The following chapters will examine four examples in which gender rights and the rights of a minority cultural community appear at odds within a larger multicultural, Western society. In each case the state, to varying degrees, has intervened without fully taking women into account. By examining these situations through the lens of gendered cultural rights, in which women's human rights to culture are addressed, the framing and resolution of this issue can change.

Chapter Two is an investigation into the Foulards Affair in France in order to engage in an examination of the perceived tension between gender and cultural rights. This investigation will ultimately show why a conception of gendered cultural rights allows for this issue to be seen as an example of women's cultural rights. Although issues such as religion, gender, and political ideology have been extensively examined in this case, analyses have focused on conflict, such as between a minority religion and the secular state, as well as between women's human rights and religion and culture. The tension between different human rights is presupposed. Not only does the perception of tension affect the manner in which scholars frame this issue, it also affects the ways in which the parties respond. The rights of women have been used as a justification to ban the headscarf in French schools. Gendered cultural rights could be used by women to support the headscarf in French schools and to connect this issue to broader women's rights claims in France.

Chapter Three analyzes the issue of divorce among Orthodox Jews, primarily in New York, and shows the impracticality of the exit option as a solution. The exit option is often suggested as a solution for members facing discrimination within a minority culture. If a larger society exists in which their rights are more likely to be protected, they should be able to leave the minority group. This has often been the counter-argument to the case of Sandra Lovelace: that she did not have to remain on indigenous lands in Canada. However, this argument assumes that 1) the rights of women would be completely protected within the larger society, and 2) women want to leave. As the investigation of the *get*, the religious divorce, will illustrate, women are not always seeking the right to leave. In this example women are using the courts and legislature to help them to remain within their communities and to not have to choose between their gender rights and membership in a religious community.

In Chapter Four, the issue of exit will be further complicated through an analysis of *Mississippi Band of Choctaw Indians v. Holyfield* and the Indian Child Welfare Act (ICWA). Here again, a woman was not interested in leaving her culture. She wanted to be able to remain; however, she sought to decide for her children a different cultural identity than her own through adoption. Under the Indian Child Welfare Act, in order to remedy past harms to indigenous peoples within the United States, the Choctaw had jurisdiction over the placement of the birth mother's children when she chose to place them for adoption. She attempted to circumvent this law to give her children to a non-Indian family. However, she wished to remain on the reservation and still to be a part of the indigenous community. The law meant to protect the survival of the culture did not fully take gender into account and did not anticipate a situation in which a woman would choose to stay but wish her children adopted out. The law appears to assume that a woman wishing to choose a different cultural identity for her children would wish to leave herself.

Chapter Five will shift the analysis to an examination of gendered cultural rights as a group claim. The Hindmarsh Island Bridge Affair in South Australia is a case in which women within an indigenous community attempt to make a group claim for cultural rights. Although cultural rights claims from indigenous people have been made successfully in Australia, this case involved only a group of women within the community and ignited significant controversy. This example appears, at first, to be a clear example of a gendered cultural rights claim. However, an in-depth analysis of the case uncovers the significant obstacles women face in invoking their rights when the existence of gendered cultural rights is not explicitly addressed in international or national law. While the lack of a mechanism to address a human rights claim adequately is a theme of previous chapters, the examination of this controversy demonstrates that, if a legal system does not take gendered human rights into account, a mechanism for addressing cultural rights may not be adequate. Furthermore, this case shows that the existence of a legal mechanism is not a guarantee of a particular outcome.

Without a concept of gendered cultural rights, the rights of women may continue to be seen in opposition to the rights of culture. Without investigating cases in depth, the complex interplay between gender and culture may remain obscure. The Conclusion will address the observations about the relationship between these rights shown throughout the chapters, and discuss the implementation of gendered cultural rights. Additionally, the implications of this work for political science and other disciplines will be addressed.

2

UNDERSTANDING A WOMAN'S RIGHT TO CULTURE: THE FRENCH HEADSCARF DEBATE

In her 1999 book *Is Multiculturalism Bad for Women?*, Susan Moller Okin references, as evidence for the claim that the accommodation of culture can be detrimental to the goal of women's rights, the French headscarf debate—a controversy which arose in France when young Muslim girls were suspended for wearing headscarves to school.[94] This controversy, known as L'affaire de foulards, the Foulards Affair, the hijab debate, or the Headscarf Affair, has sparked a debate over religious freedom, cultural rights, and gender equality, and has been the subject of diverse scholarship. Works like Okin's have focused on the dangers of cultural accommodation in society based on the continued protection of women's rights. Women's rights are characterized as in opposition to the rights of culture, and choosing to protect the human right to culture is characterized as harmful, and sometimes deadly, to women.

There is no shortage of examples of the interaction of minority religions and cultures and the larger society, especially those relating to the rights of women, and gender oppression certainly does exist worldwide. As discussed, practices such as female genital cutting or honor killings have received widespread attention, and that has been associated with the debate between gender and cultural rights. In both cases culture has been used to defend the practices, but these examples have also become part of a larger discourse within academia, human rights organizations, and the media in which the relationship between gender and cultural rights appears simple: culture is deadly to women. There are customs that appear incongruent with women's human rights because of the grave human rights concerns these practices pose, but these practices also represent a focus on the extreme conflicts that arise between women and culture.

There are other examples, though, such as the French example Okin cites, in which rights conflicts do not rise to this extreme, but in which women are forced to make an unfair choice between their gender, their

---

[94] Susan Moller Okin (1999). *Is Multiculturalism Bad for Women?* Princeton: Princeton University Press.

culture, and their religion. Scholars such as John Bowen discuss the headscarf debate in France as a symbol of the problems of a multicultural society and a challenge to French identity.[91] Dominic McGoldrick examines this debate, but extends it to all of Europe in order to propose a human rights approach to this debate.[92] The enjoyment of rights should not force the choice between aspects of identity, nor can this debate be fully captured without emphasizing the interaction of gender and culture. I intend to demonstrate through the example of the headscarf or veil debate in France the complexity of women's relationship to culture and religion. Although this case appears to confirm the incompatibility of gender and culture, in reality, it illustrates why we need a concept of gendered cultural rights. An examination of a woman's right to culture can change our approach to a seemingly intractable conflict as presented in this example from France.

The Headscarf Affair

The Foulards Affair first made headlines in 1989. It began in Creil, France, a Paris suburb, with the expulsion of three Muslim girls from a public junior high school on September 18. Against the policy of Gabriel Havez College, they had worn the Islamic headscarf, or hijab, in the classroom.[93] Samira Saidani, Leila Achaboun, and Fatima Achaboun, all members of the Maghrébin community, wished to wear headscarves to school in order to comply with the standards of proper attire for Muslim women.[94] The student population consisted of students from a variety of religious and ethnic backgrounds. Because the school was a public, secular institution, the school could not promote religion nor would the school seem to endorse any one religion over another. In the interest of maintaining this secular environment, the school principal decided headscarves could be worn in the school, but must be taken off in the classroom.[95] The girls refused to enter the classroom without the head-covering. They were suspended and then expelled from school.

---

[91] John R. Bowen (2007). *Why the French Don't Like Headscarves: Islam, the State, and Public Space.* Princeton; Oxford: Princeton University Press.

[92] Dominic McGoldrick (2006). *Human Rights and Religion: The Islamic Headscarf Debate in Europe.* Oxford; Portland, OR: Hart.

[93] Cynthia DeBula Baines (1996). "L'Affaire des Foulards—Discrimination, or the Price of a Secular Public Educational System." *Vanderbilt Journal of Transnational Law,* 29: 303.

[94] Norma Claire Moruzzi (1994). "A Problem with Headscarves—Contemporary Complexities of Political and Social Identity." *Political Theory,* 22(4): 658.

[95] Ibid., p. 657.

As school officials met with the girls' parents, as well as Maghreb community and Islamic religious leaders to discuss the issue, the incident was already having a greater impact on Creil and beyond. Other students in the city began to wear headscarves to school. The story had been picked up by the press and had become a national issue. Political forces outside of the Maghreb community and the French Islamic community began aligning on either side of the debate. The Far Right, the National Front, came out strongly opposing headscarves in school, as did several Leftists. For example, five prominent scholars (both men and women), published a letter in *Le Nouvel Observateur* calling for the teachers not to back down from their position against headscarves in the classroom.[100] While the Far Right was interested in keeping immigrant influences out of French schools and France, the Left interested itself in liberating women from the oppressive influences of religion and culture. These disparate sides of the French political world found common ground on this issue. And an equally unlikely alliance emerged in the opposite camp, where many Catholics and fundamentalist Protestants aligned with Muslims to support the wearing of religious clothing and symbols in school.[101]

Most Leftists, believing in secular education, aligned themselves against headscarves in school, which made the actions of the Socialist Education Minister more surprising. Lionel Jospin, France's Minister of Education, instructed Gabriel Havez College "to readmit the young women, even if they insisted on wearing headscarves in the classroom."[102] His instructions to school officials continued a few weeks later when he explained that while schools should not expel students for wearing headscarves or other religious dress, students should be discouraged from doing so.[103]

Although the school was ordered to readmit the students, the debate had not ended. Minister Jospin sent the case to the Council of State, the highest administrative court, for a ruling. The Council announced its ruling near the end of November and stated that while headscarves and other religious symbols were permissible, they were subject to regulation. Religious symbols that "'by their ostentatious or remonstrative character, would constitute acts of pressure, provocation, proselytizing, or propaganda,'" as well as symbols that would be detrimental to student health or

---

[100] Ibid., p. 659.

[101] Ibid., p. 658 and note 23.

[102] Ibid., p 658.

[103] Sarah V. Wayland (1997). "Religious Expression in Public Schools: Kirpans in Canada, Hijab in France." *Ethnic and Racial Studies*, 20(3): 552.

disrupt the learning and teaching environment would not be tolerated in schools.[100] For the moment, headscarves were allowed but not encouraged among students. The wording from the Council's decision suggested an uneasy response to the problem. The ruling was vague. Local officials would decide what religious symbols were "ostentatious" on a case-by-case basis.[101]

This was not the end to the headscarf debate in France. The Conservatives took power in 1993 and the new Minister of Education, Francois Bayrou, ruled headscarves to be "ostentatious" religious symbols.[102] He actually prohibited all such displays of religious affiliation, but, as Cynthia DeBula Baines reports, "no one has been, or is likely to be suspended for wearing a Christian crucifix or Jewish yarmulke."[103] At first, 2,000 girls refused to remove the headscarf at school when the ban was announced in September 1994. Protests followed, but the number of students refusing to remove the headscarf steadily decreased until the school year's end when only 115 girls had been expelled.[104] The debate in France seemed to die down for a time, but the Headscarf Affair has begun to make headlines again as the French government banned headscarves from public schools in February 2004,[105] and they remain a political and educational dilemma in England, Canada, the United States, and other European nations.

In the midst of the protests, public debates, and judicial rulings, the three girls at the center of the original controversy were nearly forgotten. Most commentators mention only their expulsion and not the terms of their readmittance to school. While the Minister's position appeared to support the girls' decision to wear the headscarf to school, Norma Claire Moruzzi points out that they were encouraged to follow the principal's original order to take off the headscarf in the classroom. Samira's family agreed with the principal's plan, but Leila and Fatima would not. They still insisted on wearing the headscarf in the classroom.[106] However, they

---

[100] Ibid., p. 553.

[101] Ibid.

[102] Ibid. In fact, Wayland reports a similar incident in Montreal, Canada in which a school principal banned a female student from wearing a headscarf under the guise of the student's protection (the principal thought her attire would incite violence).

[103] Supra n93, p. 305.

[104] Ibid., p. 307.

[105] The French government established a commission to study this issue before banning the headscarf in February 2004. See Emmanuel Terray (2004). "Headscarf Hysteria." *The New Left Review* 26: 118-127.

[106] Supra n94, p. 659.

relented after the king, Hassan II, and the spiritual leader of their native Morocco intervened.[107] Although headscarves were officially allowed in French public schools, the three girls whose actions sparked the debate would have to take off their head covering during class. There was no change for them, and school officials throughout the country still had the discretion to decide whether or not headscarves would be allowed in local schools. Even before the 1994 ban, Muslim girls were strongly pressured to remove the headscarf.

The Headscarf Affair and Religious Accommodations

The controversy over the headscarf was characterized as a debate over religious freedom versus the separation of church and state, or multicultural toleration versus assimilation. As political groups weighed in, the voices of the girls in question were lost. Although the debate appeared to be clear-cut—religious interests versus secular goals—the affair was much more complex. As a public educational institution, the Gabriel Havez College where the three girls attended school was secular and situated in an ethnically and religiously diverse community. Moruzzi points out that before the girls began wearing their headscarves to school, there had already been several incidents involving the limits of religious toleration in school. For example, the year before, several Jewish students stopped attending Friday and Saturday classes that interfered with the Sabbath. In response, the school clarified its position regarding the display of religion. "[S]tudents were expected to have regular class attendance, and [sic] students should exercise discretion in the use of signifiers of cultural difference, particularly dress."[108] The impermissibility of religious-based exemptions from school requirements is extended to religious dress. Religious symbols seemed to be as threatening to uniform secular education as religious instruction.

Separation of church and state was fundamental to French education and citizenship. Sebastian Poulter, in "Muslim Headscarves in School," sheds light on the school's response to requests for religious accommodations, and suggests that French education and citizenship has always been wrapped up in the idea of the homogeneous political citizen whose distinct

---

[107] This statement is supported by note 21 in Moruzzi's article (supra n94). However, *The Los Angeles Times* tells the story differently: in a brief article from December 3, 1989, Fatima and Leila Achaboun are said to abide by the school policy, while Samira Saidani refuses to take off her headscarf during class. See "Muslim Pupils Will Take Off Scarfs in Class." *The Los Angeles Times*, Dec. 3, 1989: A15.

[108] Supra n94, p. 657.

religion and culture exists only in his private life, not his political one.[109] However, this separation manifested itself as religious suppression in the name of equality in a multicultural, secular state. As long as schools were expected to maintain a distance from the promotion or endorsement of one religion such as Christianity, or maintain neutrality in the face of multiple sects of the same religion, it was easier to expect religion and education to exist in separate spheres of life.

Christianity, while certain sects can call their members to maintain a way of life different from that of Western society, is mostly accommodated and remains the dominant religion of the West. Liberal ideas of nationhood and the secular state developed in this environment. Although liberal ideology seemed to endorse diversity by uniting all citizens under the umbrella of secular nationalism, assimilation was obligatory. Religion had to exist in the private sphere alone. Secularism was seen as neutral, but the rise in immigration and the emergence of distinct religious and ethnic groups within the West calls this neutrality into question.

Islam asserts itself as a way of life, not just a religion, which appears in conflict with Christian-influenced notions of neutrality. Confining Islam to the private sphere in the name of a religiously neutral state can have the same effect as suppressing religious belief: oppression. Sometimes hidden, hostility towards Islam exists in contemporary India, a multiethnic and multi-religious, secular state.[110] Tahir Mahmood charges that the so-called secular law often shows Hindu bias when closely examined. The author seeks to point out the problems with secular government, which is the type so admired in the West as best for all religions. Underlying Mahmood's criticism of supposedly secular laws is the assumption that secular government as a system is biased against Muslims: he implies through his argument that secular government does not exist, that all government will hold a bias toward a particular faith or ideology.

Although Mahmood's article discusses India, not France, his points can easily be translated to the French experience. Whereas the main debate in India is between Muslims and Hindus, in France it is between Muslims and Christians. Although the headscarf is not an issue Mahmood discusses, one can see how his argument could be extended to the Headscarf Affair. Muslim girls were asked to remove their head-coverings in order to blend in with other students so their religious affiliation would not be obvious or

---

[109] Sebastian Poulter (1997). "Muslim Headscarves in School: Contrasting Legal Approaches in England and France." *Oxford Journal of Legal Studies,* 17(1): 43-74, p. 50.

[110] Tahir Mahmood. "Interaction of Islam and Public Law in Independent India." In R. S. Khare (1999). *Perspectives on Islamic Law, Justice, and Society.* Lanham; Boulder; New York; Oxford: Rowman & Littlefield Publishers, Inc.

"disruptive" to the classroom. However, the denial of religion in order to create equality can have the effect of inequality. The headscarf was an integral part of proper, modest dress for these young Muslim women. To demand the removal of the head-covering was to demand that they wear what they consider to be inappropriate attire in public. While it would not necessarily impede equality to accommodate difference in dress requirements, it would be inconsistent with the principle of equality to ban them.

Of course, behind Mahmood's attacks on the supposedly secular government lies the true intent of his argument, which is to suggest that the best form of government for an Islamic population is an Islamic government. That this government would be able to create laws beneficial to a Muslim population and promote a particular type (in Mahmood's opinion, a correct form) of Islam. This presents a problem when Muslims are a minority population. Mahmood's argument, although an excellent criticism of Western secular government, cannot fully account for the multicultural society.

A Debate over Culture

The Headscarf Affair is most often discussed as an issue of religious freedom, but that oversimplifies the issue and ignores the cultural and political components of the debate. Islam is not a homogenous religion as it is described in much of the writing about the French controversy, as well as in much of Western scholarship. Just as Christianity has multiple sects that vary in specific interpretations of religious texts, Islamic religious practice varies among Muslim communities. This is especially true of the debate over the hijab. Leila and Fatima Achaboun and Samira Saidani invoked the headscarf as a requirement of appropriate dress for Muslim women. However, not all Muslim women wear such a head-covering, and among those who do there is considerable difference of opinion about this garb. In her landmark study *Women and Gender in Islam*, Leila Ahmed contends that forms of veiling pre-existed Islam in the Middle East and co-existed in multiple cultures, such as Byzantium Christians.[111] Because veiling was a cultural practice, it varied among Islamic societies and continues to do so. Calling the headscarf a cultural practice instead of a religious one leads to both solutions and also generates more problems to understanding the Headscarf Affair in France.

Muslims in France constitute approximately five percent of the French population, but about six percent of all school-children. They are both an

---

[111] Leila Ahmed (1972). *Women and Gender in Islam: Historical Roots of a Modern Debate.* New Haven: Yale University Press, pp. 14, 18.

ethnic and religious minority because the majority of French Muslims are Maghrébin, from Algeria, Tunisia and Morocco. Although Samira Saidani, Leila Achaboun, and Fatima Achaboun chose to wear headscarves in order to comply with religious teaching, it is unclear whether this decision should be classified as religious or cultural. The girls were of North African descent, but the majority of Mahgréb women did not wear headscarves.[112] Their decision cannot be seen as purely religious or purely cultural.

Commentators have suggested an alternate explanation—politics. As Muslims became more permanent members of French society, the government attempted to stem the tide of Islamic fundamentalism.[113] The French government's attempts to de-radicalize Muslims resulted in the Council de Réflexion sur l'Islam en France. This was a fifteen-member committee officially recognized by the state as a body for religious representation, but it was unelected and unrepresentative. By 1995, it had dissolved in favor of a body that more accurately communicated the positions of the Muslim community in France.[114] However, during the early days of the Headscarf Affair it was this body that was to be the authentic voice of French Muslims. Muslim organizations such as the National Federation of Muslims in France and the Union of Islamic Organizations in France were involved in the Headscarf Affair in both the media and in the negotiations between the school and the three girls. [115] However, neither could claim to speak on behalf of French Muslims. Arguments over the authentic spokespersons and authentic beliefs and practices added to the confusion over the issue. It seemed unacceptable in the media and in the public that a variety of religious/cultural practices could exist among an ethnic and religious minority group.

Gender and Islam in the Headscarf Debate

Though the Headscarf Affair can be seen through the lenses of religious freedom, cultural toleration, and nationalism, none of these explanations fully account for why the headscarf sparked such a controversy. The debate did not involve issues of public safety as are often raised with the kirpan, or ceremonial dagger, of the Sikh, nor was the issue any of the more extensive forms of hijab such as the chador of Iran. The young girls

---

[112] Supra n99, pp. 551-552 (recounting factual background summarized in this paragraph). The Muslim girls at the center of the debate are of Moroccan and Tunisian origin. Ibid., p. 552.

[113] Many Muslims emigrated from North Africa as foreign workers and eventually established a strong community in France. See supra n97.

[114] Supra n99, p. 552.

[115] Ibid., p. 554.

were expelled for simply wearing headscarves. To understand the significance of this piece of attire is to engage much of Western feminist scholarship regarding Islam.

Feminist analysis of women in Islamic thought has often sought to show that, as in Western culture, women in Islamic thought and society have been considered different and inferior to men.[116] It is the man who is the only true member of society; therefore, the question of *what to do about the women* becomes legitimate and important. Women become appendages of men in society and potentially disruptive influences. Each man's control over the women belonging to him mirrors society's control over all men, and, through them, all women. The control of women's sexuality is key to not only the control of the female population, but also the entire society.[117] This analysis applies both to Western and Islamic cultures. These attitudes regarding the need to control and regulate women's sexuality can be found in Christianity as well as Islam. Unique to the world of Islam, though, is a synthesis of politics and religion that is the background against which all discussions of political theory and practice must be drawn.

The definition of women's status was of utmost importance during the establishment of Islam. While it did not invent customs such as the veil that regulate a woman's appearance and place in society, it did "selectively [sanction] customs already found among some Arabian tribal societies while protecting others."[118] Women's sexuality had been an issue for the

---

[116] The writings of Jean-Jacques Rousseau and Simone De Beauvoir illustrate the position of women in Western society. Rousseau's work typifies the Enlightenment thinkers' embracement of theories that empowered men with discussion of equality and freedom, yet all the while excluding women not just from these rights, but from humanity itself. Rousseau deconstructs the ideas of the sovereign, citizenship, and the formation of societies; however, he refuses to see the family and the role of women as social constructions. He assumes patriarchy and its subordination of women as natural. Conversely, Simone De Beauvoir, a twentieth century feminist theorist and existentialist, picks up on women's excise from humanity in Western society through the concept of "otherness." Men are seen as the norm for humanity and, therefore, humanness is equated with maleness, which leaves women outside of the realm of human (which obviously includes the realms of society and political discourse). See Jean-Jacques Rousseau (1762). "The Social Contract." In Isaac Krammick (Ed.) (1995). *The Portable Enlightenment Reader.* (pp. 430-441). New York: Penguin Books; Jean-Jacques Rousseau (1762), Ernest Rhys (Ed.), Barbara Foxley (Trans.) (1933). *Emile.* London: J.M. Dent & Sons Ltd; New York: EP Dutton & Co., Inc.; Simone De Beauvoir (1989), H.M. Parshley (Trans.) (1953). *The Second Sex.* New York: Vintage Books.

[117] See the diagrams representing women's place in Islam and, therefore, Islamic society on pages 71 and 72 of Fatna A. Sabbah (1984), Mary Jo Lakeland (Trans.) *Woman in the Muslim Unconscious.* New York: Pergaman Press.

[118] Leila Ahmed (1972). *Women and Gender in Islam: Historical Roots of a Modern Debate.* New Haven: Yale University Press, p. 45.

societies of the Middle East long before Islam, but, as Ahmed contends, it was able to "incorporate seamlessly an already-developed scriptural misogyny into the socio-religious universe it too would inscribe."[119] She asserts that patriarchy was institutionalized within the religion and the new society. The linchpin of the societal structure manifested itself as regulation of women's sexual freedom, which often masqueraded as protection in the rhetoric of society.

Women's dress and action are restricted for their own good and for the good of society, but feminist writers such as Fatna Sabbah see it different-ly. The controversial *Woman in the Muslim Unconscious* addresses the issue of protection versus subordination and concludes that women are regulated in the name of protection because *they* are the threat to the system, not men. She contends that while the rhetoric of Islam places the threat to women's morality on men, a closer examination of rhetoric and practice shows that it is clear that the blame is placed upon the women. Women's sexuality must be controlled or protected because men are a constant threat to women's virtue and, therefore, to society.

It is women acting outside of the societal regulations regarding sexuali-ty that threaten the system. In the patriarchal mindset, women entice men to destroy their own social creation of a society built upon the idea of the man as the citizen and believer—the human being. Woman can undo the system by virtue of her very existence as a woman because women's bodies are an invitation to self-destruction that men cannot turn down. "This destructive intelligence [of hers is] . . . devoted to the calculated, cold, and permanent destruction of the system."[120] She is depicted as possessing a sexual appetite that no one man can satisfy, which then leads her to adultery, homosexuality, prostitution, and even bestiality in the Muslim erotic discourse that Sabbah describes. The woman, in this theory, dis-dains the system and is always looking for a new way in which to destabi-lize it. Therefore, control of her must be sought at all costs in society. She must be stopped from destroying the family, the religion, and the state with her unsanctioned sex acts. For these reasons, Sabbah contends, the desired characteristics in a Muslim woman come to be immobility, lack of will, and silence.[121]

It is this explanation from Sabbah that allows a fuller understanding of the meaning of statements from Ziba Mir-Hosseini's *Gender and Islam*, in which clerics state that women are allowed participation in Islamic society

---

[119] Ibid., p. 36.

[120] Supra n117, pp. 32-33.

[121] Ibid., p. 44.

when they obey the laws created for their modesty and protection.[122] Sabbah's point is best illustrated by questions and answers from Ayatollah Azari-Qomi, a traditionalist cleric in Iran, whose work appears in excerpt form in Mir-Hosseini's book. The questioner asks the Ayatollah if women can wear clothing covering the same body parts of the hijab instead of wearing a hijab. The Ayatollah responds by saying that no, a hijab must be worn because "[women's] clothing must cover the parts which cause stimulation, in addition to covering the skin and its color."[123] He states explicitly that a woman's body causes stimulation and his answers show that she must be controlled in order to control men. Men are portrayed as helpless to stop themselves from breaking moral codes if they are confronted with contact with a woman. Her body and even her voice are to be hidden in the name of her protection, but, obviously, it is the men who are protected from her.

Women and Culture

The work of these authors fits squarely into the predominant Western feminist discourse of the patriarchy and the position of women in non-Western cultures. Susan Moller Okin, as I stated earlier, commented specifically on this French case, and has expanded her view of culture in other work. Although women, she contends, may not wish to leave their culture or may not be able to do so, Okin considers this to be a product of oppression. However, her response to this situation shows the same assumptions that women need liberation from this symbol of subordination. Okin's concern is that unchecked multiculturalism will create a human rights void in which all practices are acceptable even if they violate the rights of individuals. This can partially explain the French reaction, particularly the leftist reaction in the Headscarf Affair, but it cannot fully account for the motivations of the young girls whose chose to wear the Muslim head-covering.

Westerners have as much vested interest in suppressing the headscarf as Muslims have in promoting it. Dress is so contentious because, as Bhikhu Parekh asserts, dress in multicultural societies is the visible sign of culture.[124] However, the significance of the headscarf debate is more than

---

[122] Mir-Hosseini, Ziba (1999). *Islam and Gender: The Religious Debate in Contemporary Iran*. Princeton, NJ: Princeton University Press, p. 93.

[123] Ibid., p. 69.

[124] Bhikhu Parekh (2000). *Rethinking Multiculturalism: Cultural Diversity and Political Theory*. Cambridge, MA: Harvard University Press, p. 243. See also Alison Dundes Renteln (2004). "Visual Religious Symbols to the Law." *American Behavioral Scientist*, 47(12): 1573-1596.

outward displays of culture or religion. It is best seen as a type of symbolic politics in which women's identities defined culture. Nayereh Tohidi writes that a similar debate over female dress erupted in Azerbaijan after the fall of the Soviet Union. Muslim women and their attire were seen as the symbols of the Azerbaijan national identity and the ways in which they differed from neighboring Turkey, Iran, and Europe. Women became "keepers of the tradition."[125] Their modest appearance connoted Azerbaijan's existence between the worlds of Europe and the Muslim world. Women wear long skirts and modest outfits as a sign of their nation's independence.

The feminist scholarship does not fully investigate the meaning of culture in this debate. Because culture is seen as the institutionalization of the patriarchy, Western feminist scholars often assume culture to be universally threatening, but often focus their energies on what they perceive to be particularly problematic cultural practices found in non-Western societies. Narayan argues that even the terms "Western" and "non-Western" reinforce a colonial distinction and imply a notion of static culture.[126] The focus on saving non-Western women from culture creates resentment of Western interference in culture and makes local dissenters into outsiders because they are perceived as taking on the mindset and goals of Westerners.[127] The distrust of Western feminist agendas is important to understanding the Headscarf Affair because it shows the conflicting perspectives and goals of women from different cultural communities. The assumption that Muslim women would see the *hijab* as a symbol of subordination illustrates an inability to recognize a differing perspective from within the community. The veil can be a positive symbol of culture, and women do choose dress as an indication of culture.[128] The girls at the center of the debate chose to adopt this symbol as an outward sign of their gender and cultural and religious identities.

Although the *hijab* issue in France is not fully captured in a response emphasizing only gender rights, examining this issue through the right to culture is also problematic. The young women at the center of this case were part of an immigrant community, not a long-standing national

---

[125] Nayereh Tohidi (1996). "Soviet in Public, Azeri in Private: Gender, Islam, and Nationality in Soviet and Post-Soviet Azerbaijan." *Women's Studies International Forum*, 19(1/2): 120.

[126] Uma Narayan (1998). "Essence of Culture and a Sense of History: A Feminist Critique of Cultural Essentialism." *Hypatia*, 13(2): 86-106.

[127] Alison M. Jagger (1998). "Globalizing Feminist Ethics." *Hypatia*, 13(2): 7-31.

[128] Bahia Tahzib-Lie (2000). "Applying a Gender Perspective in the Area of the Right to Freedom of Religion or Belief." *Brigham Young University Law Review*, 2000: 967-987.

minority, which is an important distinction to many scholars.[129] More importantly, it is unclear in this example if the decision to wear the *hijab* could be considered religious or cultural. There is variance among Muslims in dress, so the choice of this particular dress is not necessarily religious. As mentioned earlier, because the young women at the heart of the original controversy did not come from families or regions where this type of dress was common, it also cannot be said to be purely cultural. As a purely religious or cultural rights claim, this example does not fit; therefore, strategies such as Bhikhu Parekh's conception of the spokesperson, cannot be completely successful. As evidenced in the French example, the identity of the spokesperson is unclear because of the cultural and religious diversity within a community that is seen as homogenous by the mainstream culture.

A Woman's Right to Culture

The Headscarf Affair in France shows the fervor with which societies debate cultural and religious rights. The young girls at the center of the debate were virtually ignored after the initial media attention. Their voices were absent from the debate. Although the authenticity of the headscarf as a religious/cultural practice of North African Muslims in France is debatable, it is clear that the girls' insistence upon wearing them presents a claim of a cultural tradition. Attending a multiethnic and multi-religious secular school in predominantly Christian France, the girls' actions can be inferred as establishing a distinct cultural identity. The girls at the center of the debate chose to adopt this symbol as an outward sign of their gender and cultural and religious identities.

Although this identity can be seen as promoting religious division and female subordination, the girls' actions can be seen as liberating because they embraced their religion and culture instead of shedding them for assimilation into French society. Okin's argument that the acceptance of cultural traditions has a negative impact on women because cultural traditions are patriarchal, is a less radical version of Sabbah. While these scholars are quick to examine the ill effects of culture on non-Western women, they do not examine the ways in which Western women are connected to culture. Missing from much of this feminist literature is the acknowledgement that Western women too are part of distinct cultural traditions.

---

[129] Will Kymlicka. *Multicultural Citizenship: A Liberal Theory of Minority Rights.* New York: Oxford University Press, p. 63.

It is only non-Western women that are asked to divest themselves of culture in the name of liberation. The assumption about the nature of women's liberation colors the entire relationship between women and culture, therefore resulting in the false dichotomy between gender and cultural rights. However, the act of liberation from oppression is not liberation if women must give up their cultural and religious identities. Women have as much right to their cultural and religious traditions as they do to gender equality, and the embracement of cultural traditions should not automatically signal women's subordination just as their denial should not be a necessary sign of female advancement.

In the example, neither religious liberty nor cultural rights are enough to explain the rights claims of the women. Furthermore, defending the schoolgirls' right to wear the headscarf is difficult using Western notions of women's human rights. It cannot be seen as purely gender discrimination. It is only through the connection of these rights that their claims can be fully understood. It allows for an account of this example that utilizes the concept of women's culture, which recognizes women's agency and their complicated identities. For women to have full access to their human rights they must be allowed to reclaim the notion of culture. The multilayered identity of women requires a re-imagining of culture in which women's roles and traditions are seen as cultural contributions and recognized as a rights category in which other rights are mutually reinforcing, instead of a point of division that allows for the characterization of women's human rights as Western.

Women chose a gendered cultural identity which conflicted with the state and could not be completely supported by culture and religion or gender. The controversy also demonstrated the problem of public policy which is based on an assumption of neutrality. The disallowance of "ostentatious" religious symbols was neutral on its face towards religion. However, the underlying assumption of the neutrality of Western dress, which has developed in an environment in which Christianity has been the predominant religion, as well as notions of assimilation and assumptions regarding women's human rights and culture, created a situation in which Muslim women were forced to choose between different aspects of their identity. Moreover, Muslim women's right to express their identity within a gendered cultural context through dress was curtailed in a manner which would impact neither mainstream men and women nor Muslim men. The law's disproportionate impact on the symbols and dress of Muslim women in France shows the need for a category of gendered cultural rights to adequately address this human rights dilemma.

3

THE *GET* AND THE EXIT OPTION IN NEW YORK

The category of gendered cultural rights is not limited to dress or cultural and religious symbols. This case study demonstrates that a gendered right to culture can be the best way to conceptualize within a human rights framework a situation with gender, religious, and cultural dimensions. This concept is also relevant in both explaining and conceptualizing solutions to human rights concerns in which women are caught in other controversies. Without the lens of a gendered cultural rights, the hijab issue in France at first glance can seem to pit the interests of women against those of the minority culture, and the state against them both.

This is true of the issue of the *get*, or religious divorce in Orthodox and Conservative Judaism. For Orthodox Jews in the United States and many other countries, divorce is a two-step process. The laws of the state require a civil divorce, but a religious divorce is also necessary.[130] However, only the husbands can grant the religious divorce. This aspect of religious law, coupled with the existence of state law, has led to the phenomenon of the *agunah*, or "chained wife": women who have obtained a civil divorce but are still considered married women in their communities. Because their husbands have not given the *get*, they cannot date, remarry, or have children without severe social and religious implications for themselves and any future offspring.

This problem exists in religious law because of the differential power of the husband and wife to divorce. This dilemma has caught the attention of community leaders, legislators, and the courts in several countries and led to proposed solutions from both inside the community and from the larger society--ranging from national legislation in Canada to protests outside the Florida workplace of the husband of an *agunah*.[131] Scholars have offered various proposals and have framed this matter as an issue of women's rights versus cultural rights or of the Establishment Clause. It has been

---

[130] The *get* is not necessary for a divorce in which the parties were married in either a civil or reform ceremony. Michelle Greenberg-Korbin (1999). "Civil Enforceability of Religious Prenuptial Agreements." *Columbia Journal of Law and Social Problems*, 32: 370.

[131] Canada Divorce Act (1990). Section 21.1; Antigone Barton. "Protesters: Doctor's Divorce Isn't Complete." *Palm Beach Post*. March 15, 2007, 1B.

seen as an issue in which the state has not done enough to intervene or as one in which the state has become too involved in purely religious matters. It can be argued that this should be a non-issue because women are free to leave their religion and community or engage in a version of their religion in which the religious divorce is not required. Women have a right of exit. However, none of the ways in which this issue is discussed fully explore the human rights concerns it raises. The main question when examining this issue is: what is the proper role of a democratic state with regard to the sexist rule of a minority religion? The situation of the *agunah* shows the complexity of the state's need to balance the rights of women with the right to religion. By looking at the *get* in New York, which has adopted legislation on this issue, I explore possible solutions and contend that the appropriate state involvement level in this human rights concern is best found by looking at the issue from the perspective of women's rights to be part of their religion.

The *Get*

The situation of the *agunah*, a Hebrew term translated as "chained wife," whose husband will not grant her the *get*, is unique to Orthodox Judaism.[132] Most members of mainstream society are not required to obtain both a civil and religious divorce in order to end a marriage. Although Catholics cannot remarry in the Catholic Church without a religious annulment of the previous marriage, this is a situation in which neither the former husband nor former wife has the power to grant it themselves. The church must do so. The issue of the *get* does not affect Reform Jews either because it is not required in this sect of Judaism.[133] The issue of the *get* limits the freedom of female members of Orthodox and Conservative Judaism.[134] They cannot force their husbands to grant the *get*, and, for women who remarry and have children without first obtaining a *get,* their children will be considered *mamzer,* which means they would be illegitimate and unable to marry other Jews.[135] The religious court, or Beth Din,

---

[132] Ester Tager (1999). "The Chained Wife." *Netherlands Quarterly of Human Rights*, 17(4): 426.

[133] Jessica Davidson Miller (1997). "The History of the Agunah in America: A Clash of Religious Law and Social Progress." *Women's Rights Law Reporter*, 19.1: 1-19. Miller notes (p. 6) that the Reform movement ceased requiring the *get* in 1869.

[134] Mostly, those affected will be members of the Orthodox community. Conservative Judaism, although a *get* is required, has taken steps to address this issue. I will discuss this in more detail.

[135] Supra n132, p. 426. Tager goes on to point out that this is not true for men. Husbands without a *get* who remarry and have children will not have children considered *mamzer.*

cannot do so nor can the state judicial system because any *get* not given voluntarily would be invalid.

The issue of the *get* is of particular concern in the United States because the law of divorce is mostly uniform, although it may vary slightly from state to state. There is no personal law in which members of a religious group have matters of family law regulated through laws applying only to members of that group. Therefore, Orthodox Jews must be divorced twice. This in and of itself is not a problem. There is no conflict between state law and religious law on this point. The problem lies in the nature of the religious divorce in Orthodox Judaism. The unequal power relationship in which only the husband may grant the divorce, coupled with the existence of a civil divorce, has created a situation in which women may obtain a civil divorce, but not a religious one. Some husbands have used the *get* to renegotiate the financial or custody arrangement from the civil divorce. A wife who refuses to make a new arrangement may remain an *agunah* for years.

Although the granting of the *get* is a religious issue, it has implications for the state. The civil divorce is sometimes used as a bargaining tool. For the state to ignore the *get,* it would be in many ways perpetuating a situation in which women cannot fully invoke their human rights. The court, often, has already ruled on a financial and custody arrangement which the *get* would allow one party to circumvent. Judicial authority is undermined in this way.

History of the *Get*

Unlike in Christianity, divorce has traditionally been possible in Judaism. There have been grounds for both husbands and wives to initiate divorce proceedings under religious law irrespective of state action, although the majority of the power to divorce has always rested with the husband. Traditionally, women have had a more limited right to initiate divorce for reasons such as infidelity.[136] If a woman is granted a divorce by the *Beth Din* for a reason such as this, the ruling is known as *kofin* and a husband has to grant the *get*. This is the only time coercive measures are allowed.[137] The religious court does not have the power to order a husband to grant the divorce.[138] This has to be done of his own free will, and ordering him to grant his wife a divorce or coercing him in some way automati-

---

[136] Supra n130, p. 365.

[137] Ibid., p. 366. A divorce ruling for a divorce initiated by a husband is known as *Yotze*.

[138] Linda S. Kahan (1985). "Jewish Divorce and Secular Courts: The Promise of Avitzur." *The Georgetown Law Journal,* 73: 199.

cally invalidates the *get*. This does not, though, mean that a husband has complete unilateral authority to divorce, because a wife has to accept the *get* before a divorce can be finalized.[139] This may seem to be a small point, these nuances must be understood to avoid oversimplification.

When divorce was handled solely within Judaism, religious divorce law, although skewed in favor of men, did provide some protection for women, so the situation of the *agunah* was not as common. The granting of the *get* was the only way for a husband to obtain a divorce. This changed with the advent of civil divorce in states.[140] The state began to apply its own divorce laws, but religious divorce was still necessary for those in the Jewish community. With this two-tiered process and the existence of a larger secular mainstream society religious divorce became more complicated.

It was then possible for a husband and wife to divorce in the eyes of the state, but still be married within the religious community. This created more problems for the wife than the husband. Also, it sometimes created an incentive for a husband to withhold the *get* from his wife if the terms of the civil divorce were not in his favor. He could use the promise of the *get* as leverage for more property or child custody rights. There have been several proposed solutions such as creating conditional marriages or modifying the marriage contract. For example, Shlomo Riskin traces the history of divorce in Jewish law and points out previously suggested solutions to the *agunah* problem, including a suggestion in France at the turn of the twentieth century that all Jewish marriages be conditional. This meant that if a couple chose to divorce civilly, then the relationship would be "nullified retroactively."[141] The concern over a couple's possible status as divorced in the wider society but married within Judaism prompted

---

[139] Supra n130, p. 364. Greenberg-Korbin points to a decree by the Rabbi Gershomides in the tenth century, which established the necessity of the wife's acceptance of the *get* in order to effect the divorce. The purpose, Greenberg-Korbin notes, is to prevent unilateral power. See also Ester Tager, supra n132. Tager notes (p. 427) that a husband can also apply to a rabbinical court for a *heter* or "permit to take another wife without the need for divorce from the first wife[.]" This is issued if the first wife is unable to receive a *get* because she has disappeared or simply refuses to accept it.

[140] Shlomo Riskin (1989). *Women and Jewish Divorce: The Rebellious Wife, the Agunah and the Right of Women to Initiate Divorce in Jewish Law, A Halckhic Solution.* Hoboken, NJ: Ktav Publishing House, p. 135. Riskin explains (pp. 134-135) why the *get* was less of a problem when Jews lived within a tight-knit Jewish community and Jewish law was the law. There was no larger society with its own seemingly neutral laws that could conflict with Jewish law.

[141] Ibid., pp. 136-137.

creative proposals such as this, but none was widely accepted as they faced opposition from within the community.

A significant attempt to address the issue of the *get* within the community came from the advent of an amendment to the *ketubah,* or traditional marriage contract within Judaism, which is signed before the wedding ceremony, within Conservative Judaism. The Saul Lieberman addition to the *ketubah* was an attempt to resolve this issue within the community. This amendment attempts to remedy this problem through the stipulation in the marriage contract that the parties, the husband and wife, are bound by the Rabbinical Assembly Beth Din. Therefore, if the Beth Din ruled that a husband should present his wife with a *get*, he would be bound to do so.[142] Although refusing to grant the *get* would still be possible because it would still have to be a voluntary action, the Beth Din could impose a financial penalty.[143] The monetary penalty would not be coercion. It would be an incentive for the husband to do what he had promised in the *ketubah*.

This amendment was incorporated into the *ketubah* in Conservative Judaism, but Orthodox Judaism has rejected it because the marriage contract is a religious document, which should not be used as a contract enforceable in civil courts.[144] This solution offered some benefits, but there are drawbacks as well. The Beth Din may not always be the best venue for divorce settlement proceedings. Although this solution would most likely prevent the continued phenomenon of the civilly divorced but religiously married couples in which the husband refuses to grant the *get*, leaving the state out, for the most part, of the divorce settlement This may not always be in the best interest of either party, especially women. Women may want to take advantage of the divorce laws and protections of the state court, just as they may want to be able to enjoy life within their religious and cultural community. This solution seemed to offer protection for the minority culture, but does not necessarily protect women's human rights or their human right to be full participants within their cultures.

The *Get* and New York

Although the *get* and the situation of the *agunah* are not new issues in the United States, there is no national legislative or judicial approach to

---

[142] Ibid., p. 137.

[143] Ibid.

[144] Ibid., p. 136.

this issue.[145] It is largely unknown in many parts of this populous, multicultural country. However, although the federal government has not addressed this issue, some states have been forced to confront it in courts or in the proposal of legislation. None have approached this matter as comprehensively as New York, where both the judiciary and the legislature have crafted approaches to the *get*. [146]

The New York judiciary first dealt with this issue. Divorce among Orthodox and Conservative Jews, like divorce among most Americans, has become more prevalent. Some of the early cases to reach the courts "[i]nvolved specific agreements between couples, usually as part of a written separation agreement, that stated the spouses' desire for a religious divorce."[147] Courts were asked to enforce a civil agreement, which the parties had undertaken as part of their divorce proceedings. There was never a religious question because the courts were not asked to interpret religious law or to even order a husband to give his wife the *get* against his will because the husband had agreed to do so in the settlement.

However, the most important judicial decision in New York regarding the *get* is *Avitzur v. Avitzur*. Boaz and Susan Avitzur married in 1966 in a traditional Conservative ceremony, with the *ketubah* including the provision that disputes be settled in the religious court.[148] They did not have any children. Susan Avitzur was granted a civil divorce from her husband in 1978. However, her husband would not grant a religious divorce nor would he appear before the Beth Din. She filed suit for the enforcement of the *ketubah* in New York court claiming Boaz Avitzur was in breach of contract.[149] The trial court ruled in Susan Avitzur's favor, but the decision was reversed on appeal. The New York Court of Appeals ruled in a 4–3 decision

---

[145] Canada has addressed the issue of the *get*. See Ontario Family Law Act 1986 and Canada Divorce Act 1990 Supra n131. See Marvin E. Jacob. "The Agunah Problem and the So-Called New York State Get Law: A Legal and Halachic Analysis." In *Women in Chains: A Sourcebook on the Agunah*. Ed. Jack Nusan Porter. Northvale, NJ: Jason Aronson Inc. 1995: pp. 169-170. Jacob notes that, under Canadian law, a husband must grant the *get* within fifteen days of his wife's demand or risk losing completely in the divorce proceedings. Tager is critical of the Canadian approach because of the Halakhic problems with it. Supra n132, p. 448.

[146] New Jersey has also had cases before its judiciary regarding the *get*. See Marc Feldman (1990). "Jewish Divorce and Secular Courts: Helping a Jewish Woman Obtain a Get." *Berkeley Women's Law Journal*, 5: 141, at p. 150. See also *Minkin v. Minkin*, 180 N.J. Super. 260, 434 A.2d 665 (1981).

[147] Supra n137, p. 211.

[148] Supra n138, p. 198.

[149] David Margolick. "Court Rules New York Can Enforce Jewish Marriage Contract." *The New York Times*, Feb. 16, 1983: B1.

in 1983 that the *ketubah* was legally binding.[150] Susan Avitzur won and her husband was required to go before the Beth Din. The Court did not require Mr. Avitzur to grant his wife the *get*, but only to appear before the religious court, which he had already agreed to in the document signed at the marriage ceremony.

This decision has been praised and criticized for the use of the courts of New York State in examining a religious matter.[151] In the dissent, Justice Jones writes that this decision is problematic under the Establishment Clause.[152] However, there are several points that are important to note. The distinguishing feature of this decision is the use of the *ketubah* as an enforceable contract in the state of New York.[153] However, Susan Avitzur did not argue that the court should force her husband to grant her the *get*. It would have been against her own interests to do so because the religious divorce degree she procured would be considered invalid within her community. She would not have been able to remarry in an Orthodox or Conservative ceremony. Any future children would be considered illegitimate and they would be barred from marrying other Jews.[154] Instead of asking the court to rule that her husband give her the *get*, she asked that the court enforce the *ketubah* as a prenuptial contract and require her husband to appear before the Beth Din.

Civil courts are often asked to examine prenuptial agreements and enforce the terms of contracts. However, this was different because the contract was symbolic as well. It is often written in Aramaic with an English translation and, is highly decorative.[155] Unlike other antenuptial agreements, it is a ceremonial document and not a legal one. Applying contract law to a ceremonial religious document could, as was the dissent's

---

[150] *Avitzur v. Avitzur*, Court of Appeals of New York, 58 N.Y.2d 108, 446 N.E.2d 136, 459 N.Y.S.2d 572 (1983). New York's "Court of Appeals" is the state's highest court.

[151] Elizabeth Lieberman criticized the decision in *Avitzur v. Avitzur* in a 1983 Note because of First Amendment concerns. Enforcing a religious document in court and ordering parties to a religious court, conflicts with the Establishment Clause, for Lieberman, because the state will become entangled with religion. Lieberman, Elizabeth (1983). "*Avitzur v. Avitzur*: The Constitutional Implications of Judicially Enforcing Religious Agreements." *The Catholic University Law Review*, 33: 242.

[152] Ibid., p. 440.

[153] Supra n138, p. 213.

[154] Tager points out that even though the *get* is considered a problem for people within Jewish communities where a *get* is considered a requirement for divorce, it can also be a problem for children of second marriages whose parents did not seek a *get*. These children could be considered *mamzerim*. Supra n132, p. 438.

[155] Feldman, supra n146, p. 141.

view, constitute entanglement with religion.[156] Not all Jewish marriage contracts contained the relevant clause used in *Avitzur v. Avitzur* and therefore could not all be used in a similar fashion in divorce proceedings. The criticism of the use of a religious marriage document in a state court proceeding raises questions about the relationship between religion and the state. This criticism, though, implies that the use of the *ketubah* in this case was substantially different than in other cases courts have undertaken.

Although differences exist between the *ketubah* and a standard prenuptial agreement, this case was not the first in which American courts have been forced to weigh in on marriage contracts and ceremonies which differ from those commonly found in the United States. Ann Laquer Estin's study of "Pluralism in American Family Law" gives an overview of the ways in which American law clashes with religious law in the area of divorce. American courts are not addressing these issues in an overly organized fashion, though, because each case presents new challenges.[157] The American legal system is secular, but issues of family law, Estin notes, especially those from minority cultures, require courts to examine religious matters.[158] Alison Dundes Renteln, in her 2004 book *The Cultural Defense*, proposes that courts be able to take culture into account when deciding cases. She notes several cases in which courts have dealt with religious and ethnic minorities whose culturally-motivated action has often led to conflicts with the American legal system, including issues of marriage and divorce.[159] Courts cannot avoid issues relating to religion and culture. Even with regard to the *get*, Jessica Miller points out that New York first encountered this issue in a 1917 case regarding inheritance.[160]

Even though the decision in *Avitzur* showed that courts could enforce the *ketubah*, it did not solve the problems of the *agunah*. Not every *ketubah* contains that clause, so not all women in this situation could avail

---

[156] Supra n138, pp. 216-217.

[157] Ann Laquer Estin (2004). "Embracing Tradition: Pluralism in American Family Law." *Maryland Family Law*, 63: 540-604.

[158] Ibid., p. 542.

[159] Alison Dundes Renteln (2004). *The Cultural Defense*. New York: Oxford University Press.

[160] Supra n133, p. 4. In the case of *In re Spondre*, Moses Spondre sought to stop Rachel Spondre from administering the will of his son, Henry. Rachel Spondre claimed to have divorced her first husband, who had disappeared, and married Henry before arriving in the United States. Moses Spondre claimed she had never received a divorce from her first husband. Miller points out that Rachel Spondre wins most likely due to poor translation of Moses Spondre's testimony and the lack of understanding on the part of the judge regarding the *get*. See *In re Spondre*, 98 Misc. 524 (Surrogate's Court, New York County, 1917).

themselves of the same option.[161] Even for women who did ask the court to enforce the *ketubah*, it only requires that the husband appear before the Beth Din. The rabbinical court cannot demand that a husband grant his wife a religious divorce if he does not want to do so. The justices in this decision attempted to walk a fine line between engaging in the internal rules of a minority group and the need to protect all citizens of society. The success of this decision is that it acknowledges that there are implications for the state of the internal rules of the minority group that requires the religious divorce.

However, the New York court would not rule that a husband's refusal to grant a religious divorce to his wife was actionable. Charles Perl and Chana Perl divorced in 1982. The court made a property settlement, but they entered into a new arrangement four days later, in which Chana Perl gave virtually all property and an additional financial settlement to Charles Perl. In return, she received a *get*. Immediately, she and her uncle stopped payment on their checks and Charles Perl sued.[162] Chana Perl argued that she had been coerced into the financial agreement as the only way to receive a religious divorce.[163] The court held in the 1987 decision that the refusal itself to grant the *get* was not actionable.[164] The court could not order someone to grant the *get*. Therefore, an *agunah*, although she could possibly have her husband instructed by a New York court to appear before the religious court, could not have the New York judiciary order her husband to grant a *get* or sue for his refusal to grant it.

These two decisions are significant because they show the willingness of the court to examine a religious situation and order a person to appear before a tribunal other than that organized by the state. In so doing, it recognized religious authority. Further, it also recognized that refusing to intervene in this situation under the guise of the neutrality of the secular state would have a disproportionately negative impact on an Orthodox Jewish woman.

---

[161] For example, Kent Greenawalt cites an Arizona decision in which the Court of Appeals did not find the *ketubah* sufficient to order the husband to give a *get*. This *ketubah* was general. It contained no specific provisions for the *get*. Kent Greenawalt (1998). "Religious Law and Civil Law: Using Secular Law to Assure Observance of Practices with Religious Significance." *Southern California Law Review*, 71: 819.

[162] *Perl v. Perl*, 126 A.D.2d 91, 512 N.Y.S.2d 372, 374, 126 A.D.2d 91 (1987).

[163] Ibid., 512 N.Y.S.2d at 374.

[164] Ibid. Justice Wallach feared allowing a claim based on the denial of the *get* because of issues of the separation of church and state. Ibid., p. 376.

The New York Legislative Response

While the courts were dealing with the issues surrounding the *get* in cases like *Avitzur,* there were also those who wished the legislature to intervene. Agudat Israel of America, for example, lobbied the New York legislature to enact a solution to the *agunah* problem.[165] Following this decision and other cases involving the *get,* the New York state legislature amended the Domestics Relations Law in 1983 to address this issue. Section 253 states that a person filing for divorce in New York state must "certify that he or she has taken or that he or she will take prior to the entry of final judgment, all steps solely within his or her power to remove any barrier to the defendant's remarriage following the annulment or divorce[.]"[166] The language is both gender and religious neutral. In theory, this section of the statute could apply to anyone filing for a civil divorce.

However, it is irrelevant to most citizens in New York. For example, Protestants have no requirements and no method of receiving a religious divorce. Catholics must have an annulment approved by the church before a new marriage can be recognized there, but neither party to divorce proceedings has the power to do this. Although the barrier to remarriage applies to both Orthodox men and women in civil divorce, it is still the case that only men have the power to grant the divorce. The duty to end the religious marriage is theirs. This addition to the Domestic Relations Law is meant specifically for Orthodox husbands. A husband filing for divorce may not have the civil divorce granted until he has granted the *get.*

This addition to the Domestic Relations law received wide acceptance in the Orthodox community.[167] This solution would keep husbands who wish a civil divorce from using the religious divorce as a tool for bargaining because they would not be able to attain their goal of divorce without granting the *get.* The state's judicial system, then, cannot be used to for this purpose. This law also circumvents the problem of coercion because husbands are not coerced. They have filed for civil divorce. They no longer wish to be married.

Although accepted in the Orthodox community where the *agunah* situation is most problematic, there was not a consensus within Judaism. Members of the Reform movement offered a criticism, namely that this statute violates the Establishment Clause of the Constitution and promotes too much entanglement with religion.[168] The solution, they argued, would

---

[165] Ibid., p. 374.

[166] New York Domestic Relations Law § 253.2.

[167] Supra n145, p. 162.

[168] Supra n133, p. 12.

not be found in courts or the legislature, but within the religious community.[169] The constitutional concerns with this statute, as well as the deficiencies in this solution, have been the focus of criticism from some parts of Judaism as well, from those who believe the government should not allow religious accommodations. The statute is written as religiously and gender neutral, but it treats Jews differently than other religious groups in filing for divorce.[170]

Even for supporters, the 1983 *get* law leaves much to be desired, though. The law only addresses one scenario in which a civil divorce and religious divorce would occur. It only addresses actions by the plaintiff. The situation in which a wife files for divorce, like in the case of Susan Avitzur, is left unaddressed in the law. Similarly, the case in which a woman wishes to obtain a *get* even though she was not married within an Orthodox ceremony, but became Orthodox later, or in which her second marriage would be Orthodox or Conservative, is not addressed. The law, while well intentioned, does nothing for these women.

New York's Second *Get* Law

The 1983 law, although criticized in some circles for possible problems with Establishment Clause, remains in effect, but it was not enough to solve the problem. The state was still involved in the perpetuation of the *agunah* situation because of the narrow nature of the law. In 1992, New York amended its laws again.[171] This time, the courts could take coercion into account when dividing property. Under this amendment regarding the division of property, "any decision made pursuant to this subdivision the court shall, where appropriate, consider the effect of a barrier to remarriage[.]"[172] A man was still not forced or ordered to grant his wife a *get*. This would make the religious divorce invalid and constitute too much involvement on the part of the state. Instead, the circumstances of the granting of the *get* could be taken into account, like other factors, under the law.

The application of the law is best seen in the case of *Schwartz v. Schwartz*. This was a long and convoluted divorce. Mr. and Mrs. Schwarz married in 1966 and Mrs. Schwartz filed for divorce and was granted one

---

[169] Ibid.

[170] Supra n138, pp. 203-204.

[171] Supra n145, p. 163. There is a long legislative history to this law. It had first been introduced eight years before. Jacob notes in note 11 of his article that before its passage, several rabbis were contacted regarding this bill. However, no criticism was given.

[172] New York Domestic Relations Law Art. 13, § 236, Part B, 5(h).

in 1991.[173] At the time of the divorce, they had no minor children. Mrs. Schwartz's parents, Irene and Sydney Klass, owned the *Jewish Press*, where, for the majority of the marriage, Mr. Schwartz had worked in management while Mrs. Schwartz remained home with the children. Although Mr. Schwartz had quit the *Jewish Press* for a time when the couple first moved to Israel, he was again employed there before their return to New York and after. Following their separation in 1989, Mr. Schwartz was fired. Mrs. Schwartz then began working for the *Jewish Press*.

The majority of their assets actually belonged to the *Jewish Press* or came from there.[174] The main asset in question in their divorce was the ownership of the *Jewish Press*. In 1974 they had shares of the corporation reissued so that they would have twenty-six shares and each of their two adult daughters would have twenty-four. However, they did not give their daughters the shares until 1983, and the shareholder's agreement contained a provision for buyback of the shares in which a value of $500 was placed on the stock.[175] Mr. Schwartz, the defendant in this case, claimed the stock as marital property and as a twenty-four percent ownership of the corporation.[176]

At the time of the civil divorce, Mrs. Schwartz had not received a *get* from her husband. The original *get* statute was no help to her in obtaining one in this situation because she had initiated divorce proceedings and she was not the party with the power to do away with any barriers to remarriage. The precedent set in *Avitzur v. Avitzur* could not help her either. The *Avitzur* decision depended upon the court's ability to enforce a clause in the *ketubah* as a contractual obligation, for a husband to appear before the religious tribunal. As Orthodox Jews, the *ketubah* from their wedding ceremony did not contain the clause found in those in the Conservative branch.

When the court is charged with determining the equitable distribution of assets, the issue of the *get* and the circumstances under which Mrs. Schwartz received it were considered. Mrs. Schwartz had eventually received a *get* in Israel in October of 1992. However, before she received it, she had given her former husband part of the farm in Israel and paid his legal expenses in New York and Israel. The Court determined that the

---

[173] *Schwartz v. Schwartz*, 235 A.D.2d 468, 652 N.Y.S.2d 616 (1997) (affirming), and lower court opinion cited therein. See *Schwartz v. Schwartz*, 153 Misc.2d 789 (March 11, 1992).

[174] Ibid.

[175] Ibid.

[176] Ibid.

husband's actions regarding the *get* should be taken into account in this way because, under the 1992 law, these circumstances could be considered one of the factors affecting the property settlement.[177]

The strength of the 1992 law, though, is that it attempts to address one of the holes in the first *get* legislation: a divorce initiated by a wife. As the Schwartz case shows, Mrs. Schwartz filed for divorce, but Mr. Schwartz withheld the *get*. If he had begun divorce proceedings, he would have had to remove "any barriers to remarriage," but because Mrs. Schwartz filed, he was not required to do so. This contributed to their protracted settlement litigation. The 1992 law, as used in this case, provided some remedy to the situation and recognized the existence of unfavorable financial, property, or custody agreements women felt compelled to enter into in order receive the *get*. The court has an interest in addressing this because the settlements and agreements reached under New York law were sometimes used as a basis for this negotiation. Through this law, the court was now able to address the dealings made in the shadow of the law under sometimes less than favorable circumstances. The courts do not have to turn a blind eye to financial settlements wives have made under duress.

The Orthodox Community Response

Although there has been wide consensus in the Orthodox community regarding the first *get* statute,[178] this was not true of the 1992 law. This time there had not been wide support. The Orthodox community had not supported this measure because there was disagreement within the community on whether or not this amendment would violate religious law.[179] Some groups like Agudat Israel argue that connecting the *get* to financial matters takes away from the voluntary nature of it and, therefore, could invalidate a *get* given under these circumstances.[180] Some scholars, such as Michael Broyde, have raised questions about the validity of the 1992 law and generally oppose state intervention. However, Broyde notes that the law affects very few people and that many of these divorces may still be

---

[177] Supra n173. In 1997, Mr. Schwartz appealed the decision regarding the ownership of the *Jewish Press*. He lost. *Schwartz v. Schwartz*, Supreme Court of New York, Appellate Division, 235 A.D.2d 468, 652 N.Y.S.2d 616 (1997). A more recent case dealing with this statute is *Giahn v. Giahn*, N.Y. Supreme Court, App. Div. (unreported decision, April 4, 2000).

[178] Supra n157, p. 581.

[179] Ibid., p. 582.

[180] Supra n136, p. 374.

valid.[181] Although the purpose of this law was to address the concerns which continued to arise even after the earlier statute, without fully understanding the *get* issue or considering how this law would impact Orthodox Jewish women, the group the seemingly neutral law was meant to protect, Ann Laquer Estin notes that a possible negative consequence of this statute could be to "discourage observant Jewish women from pursuing divorce proceedings in the civil courts."[182]

There have been objections to the 1992 law and concerns, more generally, about state intervention. However, everyone acknowledges that the situation of the *agunah* is an issue deserving attention. Suggested solutions which seek to solve both of these problems center around the prenuptial agreement. Another solution proposed by Rabbi Emanuel Rackman and Rabbi Moshe Morgenstern has been to grant annulments to women instead of divorces. However, they had several opponents because these annulments may not be valid under religious law.[183] Prenuptial agreements are often cited as the best way to ensure an end to the *agunah* problem.[184] The religious divorce issue will then be before a religious court. The prenuptial agreements could be enforced in civil courts, but, as in the Avitzur case, the court would not be deciding religious law. They would be enforcing contracts to which both parties had agreed and not regulating a religious practice.

Get Laws and the Establishment Clause

Several commentators have taken issue with New York's *get* statutes because they are not religiously neutral and promote entanglement with religion.[185] The neutrality of the state is threatened when religion-specific laws are enacted. Other commentators, while recognizing the dangers of entanglement, defend the statute as an accommodation of religious difference and not a promotion of one religion over another.[186] However, this is

---

[181] Michael J. Broyde (2001). *Marriage, Divorce and the Abandoned Wife in Jewish Law: A Conceptual Understanding of the Agunah Problems in America.* Hoboken, NJ: Ktav Publishing House, pp. 116-117.

[182] Supra n157, p. 582.

[183] Nadine Brozan. "Rabbis Stir Furor by Helping 'Chained Women' to Leave Husbands." *The New York Times*, Aug. 13, 1998: B1.

[184] Supra n136, p. 361.

[185] See Feldman, supra n155; Greenawalt, supra n161; and Lawrence Marshall (1986), "The Religion Clauses and Compelled Religious Divorces: A Study in Marital and Constitutional Separations." *Northwestern University Law Review*, 80(1): 204-258.

[186] Tanina Rostain (1987). "Permissible Accommodations of Religion: Reconsidering the New York *Get* Statute." *Yale Law Journal* 96: 1168. Rostain argues (p. 1150) that state "accommo-

not a gender or religiously neutral problem. The *agunah* situation usually arises when a husband refuses to grant the *get*. The law is meant to target a specific group because this is the group impacted by this issue.

The existence of divorce under state law, it could be argued, actually has a role in the perpetuation of the *agunah* phenomenon because it creates the two-step divorce process in Orthodox and Conservative Judaism, in which the state only acknowledges the existence of one of the steps. The unequal divorce power of men and women within Judaism is worsened because of the civil divorce, after which a husband may still withhold the religious divorce.[187] Without state law acknowledging this situation and attempting to provide a remedy, Orthodox women have disproportionately less power to divorce in the state than do women from the majority culture or other religious or cultural minorities with different divorce customs.

A focus on the Establishment Clause of the U.S. Constitution obscures the human rights issues of protecting the rights of female members of minority communities, as well as ignores the issue of the meaning of neutrality, which accompanies all issues of accommodation. The supposed neutrality of the Establishment Clause and the doctrine of the separation of church and state may seem an attractive method for maintaining uniform law and order in a multicultural and multi-religious society, but it is not. Laws and social custom develop in a society according to the majority culture. In the United States, our society developed in the context of Christianity. Because there is no religious divorce for Christians, the existence of civil divorce was not problematic. Separating religion and the legal system in this context posed no dilemmas. When neutrality on the part of the state is constructed in this manner and we examine the issue of the *get,* observant Jewish women will always lose. Without law that acknowledges difference, inequality will persist.[188]

---

dation of religion as legislation that functions to remove governmentally imposed burdens on religious exercise" is acceptable.

[187] Supra n138, p. 201. Linda Kahan contends that "[t]he interaction of Jewish and secular divorce law aggravates the problem inherent in Judaism's reliance on the male. When family law was the prerogative of religious communities, a couple married in a Jewish ceremony could not be divorced, even in the eyes of the state, except as sanctioned by Jewish law. Today, the state declares a couple to be divorced without regard to Jewish law." Similarly, Kent Greenawalt asserts that this situation with the *get* is not wholly the fault of religious law or civil law. The problem exists in religious law because of the differential power of the husband and wife in the divorce. However, "the state exacerbates the difficulties" through the enactment of uniform civil divorce. Supra n161, p. 830.

[188] This is the basis for the notion of differentiated citizenship, which comes from debates in the multiculturalism literature in political theory. See Will Kymlicka (1995). *Multicultural Citizenship: A Liberal Theory of Minority Rights.* New York: Oxford University Press. See

The Problem of Creating a Solution

If one accepts that the laws of the state are not neutral in impact and different solutions are necessary for different groups in order to assure equal protection under the law, the problem remains of how to achieve this. The complaints regarding the second *get* statute involve problems with the Establishment Clause and also some concerns over state interference in religious matters. This approach in New York is one solution, but countries with similar concerns have attempted to address this issue as well.

By comparison, Ontario's law is much stricter than that of New York. Under *The Family Law Act*, a husband has ten days to grant the *get* after the wife's demand. If he does not comply, he loses all claims to custody, support, and other relevant matters in the civil divorce proceeding.[189] This act, a more strict combination of both New York laws, more clearly addresses the issue of the *get* in divorce proceedings, but, unlike the New York legislative approaches, it demands compliance. This demand, while possibly necessary to ensure that a couple's civil divorce coincides with the religious divorce, runs counter to the tenets of the religious divorce, as a husband must grant the *get* of his own freewill. In comparison, the New York solutions do not seem as harsh nor do they require as much entanglement with religion. This Canadian approach, though, does attempt to stop the creation of an *agunah* by imposing a short timeline for the granting of the *get* and imposing stiff penalties for non-compliance. However, any true solution to this problem would have to be one which those within the affected minority community would accept.

The New York judicial and legislative solutions attempt to be more sympathetic on this point. The *Avitzur* decision, using the Conservative *ketubah*, does not order the *get,* but orders the husband to appear before the Beth Din. This decision can be hailed as one in which the courts used their judicial authority only to allow this matter to be settled within the community. Several scholars and religious leaders have advocated settling divorces within the Beth Din. Because courts are only directing people to fulfill contractual promises to deal with the issue within the religious community, it avoids many of the issues of separation between church and state which plague the legislative solutions.

This is more difficult than it may seem. Judaism is not a homogeneous culture or religion. There are differences between Orthodox, Conservative,

---

also Christian Joppke and Steven Lukes (Eds.) (1999). *Multicultural Questions*. New York: Oxford University Press.

[189] Supra n132, p. 447.

and Reform Jews much like there are differences between different branches of Christianity or Islam. The existence of religious and cultural difference among those who are in the majority in society is usually unquestioned. The differences among those in a minority are often perplexing to the majority, who expect the minority to speak with a singular and uncomplicated voice. If this were true in the case of the *get*, it would make the state response easier to craft and the will and needs of the minority easier to determine.

There is no central authority for Judaism who can be called upon as the representative of the group or the final authority on matters of religious law. Religious courts around the world may operate on slightly different principles, and there is no hierarchical structure, as there may be for Roman Catholics, for example. There is no expectation in mainstream society for all Christians to speak with a unified voice. However, the lack of a central rabbinical court does pose problems for assessing the authority of the Beth Din relative to a New York court.

Accommodation or Exit

Recognizing that the religious community may not necessarily fully protect women's rights either further complicates this issue. An already convoluted legal and legislative history of the *get* in New York begs the question: why do women not leave? They are divorced in the eyes of the state. The religious divorce is not necessary for all Jews. Without the *get* they would still be able to remarry in a Reform ceremony, but that would require women to change their religious beliefs. There are social implications to being an *agunah* extending to future relationships and children. More importantly, women should not have to choose between different aspects of their identities in order to enjoy their human rights.

A Critique of Ayelet Shachar's Approach

For women unable to obtain a *get* and caught between religious and state law, Ayelet Shachar has used the *agunah* situation as an example in her work regarding the status of women who are both citizens of a multicultural state and members of a minority culture. For Shachar, women may be especially vulnerable in minority groups because the laws and traditions of that community may conflict with more gender-neutral laws of the state.[190] However, Shachar acknowledges "women may still find value and meaning in their cultural tradition and in continued group mem-

---

[190] Ayelet Shachar (2000). "The Puzzle of Interlocking Power Hierarchies: Sharing the Pieces of Jurisdictional Authority." *Harvard Civil Rights-Civil Liberties Law Review*, 35: 397.

bership."[191] With a focus on family law, she points out that groups "have used marriage and divorce regulation in the same way that modern states have used citizenship law[.]"[192] Marriage and divorce are ways in which group membership is decided and maintained.

The setting of membership rules, however, is often done in ways that limit the rights of women. She terms this the "paradox of multicultural vulnerability," in which the societal attempt to accommodate a minority culture results in more problems for certain individuals within the minority group.[193] However, if the group were to be forced by the state to change its membership rules, then that would take away the authority of the group. These are both issues in which the state and the minority culture seem to be at odds over the protection of women's rights. The solution she proposes to this dilemma, using the situation of the *agunah* as an example,[194] would create a system in which the state would assume authority over a matter such as divorce when the minority group has not provided an acceptable internal solution.[195] The possibility of state action would be an incentive for minority cultures to create internal remedies, as well as provide women with a venue for their claims. This type of joint governance she terms transformative accommodations, in which neither the group nor the government has complete authority.[196]

Although her solution acknowledges the issue of gender in the relationship between the minority group and the state, Shachar does not frame this as a human rights concern. Furthermore, Shachar's transformative accommodations approach would not be a complete solution. If women and men have cultural rights that are not always the same, we should also acknowledge that that the relationship between the mainstream society and minority religions and cultures is not simplistic. The United States, for example, is more pluralistic than is often acknowledged. Even among Christians, the predominant religion, there is not uniformity. Evangelical Christians have different policy concerns, as well as cultural and religious

---

[191] Ibid., p. 398.

[192] Ibid., p. 394.

[193] Ibid., p. 386.

[194] Ayelet Shachar (2001). *Multicultural Jurisdictions: Cultural Differences and Women's Rights.* Cambridge, UK: Cambridge University Press, p. 133. Shachar explains how transformative accommodation would apply the issue of the *get*. Recognizing the role that rules and procedure play in constituting the negotiations between parties in a divorce, Shachar does not want to leave the issue of the religious divorce outside the bounds of state control because of the possibility that women will feel coerced into a disadvantageous settlement.

[195] Supra n194, pp. 134-135.

[196] Ibid., pp. 126, 128.

issues, than Roman Catholics. For example, Ash Wednesday may be an important religious day for many Christian sects who include specific religious traditions, but it is not celebrated by all groups. Differing traditions among members of a larger group such as Christians or Jews does not negate culture or religion, but shows the variability. This is another reason governments should refrain from delving too deeply into culture and religion because government attempts at regulation can be overbroad.

The *Get* through the Lens of Human Rights

In the United States, New York has grappled with the issue of the *agunah* and the proper response from the state. Unlike Canada, where federal legislation exists and the Canadian Supreme Court has taken up the issue, the United States has not approached this issue from a national perspective. Although in 2007 both Maryland and Florida considered legislation similar to that of New York, bills in both states failed.[197] The lack of a national response is problematic, because this human rights concern for women is not being fully addressed. The ultimate change for a gender-discriminatory divorce practice would have to come from within the community for them to consider it valid, but laws like those in New York are helpful because they attempt to ensure that the state will not be a party to the creation of more *agunot* without attempting to regulate religion.

As a matter of human rights, women have a right to be part of their culture, but the cultural rights of women and the special challenges they may face in invoking these rights has not been addressed in international human rights law. *The Convention on the Elimination of All Forms of Discrimination against Women* does not address the right to culture. Article 27 of the *International Covenant on Civil and Political Rights* protects the right of minorities "in community with the other members of their group, to enjoy their own culture, to profess and practice their own religion, or use their own language."[198] Although the treaty does not address gender, a woman's right to be part of her culture has been

---

[197] Jennifer Skalka. "Jewish Divorce Bill Defeated." *The Baltimore Sun*, March 17, 2007: B5; see 2007 MD H.B. 324; 2007 FL H.B. 469.

[198] United Nations (1966). *International Covenant on Civil and Political Rights*. In Ian Brownlie (Ed.) (1995). *Basic Documents in International Law, 4th ed.* Oxford: Clarendon Press, pp. 276-297, Article 27.

acknowledged in the Sandra Lovelace case before the Human Rights Committee.[199]

Although the issue of the *get* is a religious one, it is important to examine the state's proper role. Because the religious divorce must be given voluntarily, if the state law or judiciary compels the *get,* its validity would be in question. This is the concern over statutes such as that of Canada, which mandates the maximum number of days to deliver the *get* after a civil divorce. However, for the state to not intervene at all would be to turn a blind eye to situation of many women who have received a divorce in the eyes of the state but are unable to divorce within their religion. Women awaiting the *get* would violate their religious tenets to date or remarry without receiving a religious divorce. It should be noted that, although women have sought change from within religion through non-governmental organizations dedicated to the *agunah,* they also turned to the legal system for protection.

Framing the issue of the *get* as an issue of women's right to culture shows not only the necessity of some state involvement, but also the necessity of the state not intervening in the actual practices of a religious or cultural minority. In the case of the *get,* ordering a husband to give his wife a religious divorce would make it invalid. Such a law may not help women because, if the resulting divorces were deemed invalid by religious authorities, their situation would not change. They would still require a valid, voluntary religious divorce from their husbands. Looking at such a law from the perspective of women's cultural rights, the state would not have helped women fully invoke their human rights because they could still be left with an unfair choice of leaving their religion or staying with no protection of their cultural rights.

Without any involvement from the state, women would again not be able to fully enjoy their right to culture and religion. There would be no recourse from the state when, after a civil divorce, they were unable to obtain a *get.* Although the state did not create the sex discrimination within the religious divorce laws the existence of civil divorce laws, especially those that do not have any provisions regarding the religious divorce, leave women in a precarious position. For example, one Florida woman's former husband refused to give her a *get* even though he had remarried and divorced again in the ten years since their divorce.[200] Without the legal recourses available to women in New York, the options for other American

---

[199] *Sandra Lovelace v. Canada* (1981). Communication No. R.6/24. Views of the Human Rights Committee. Report of the Human Rights Committee, Annex XVIII. General Assembly Official Records, 36th Session, Supplement No. 40 (A/36/40). New York: United Nations.

[200] Supra n131.

women in this situation are social and financial. These methods can be successful, but they are all women have available without access to courts.

If women have the right to be part of their cultures, and states should protect the right to culture, that does not always mean that states have no involvement in a minority culture or are overly involved. The protection of women's cultural rights is fraught with the potential for over- or under-involvement in a minority community. To protect the right to culture and women's rights in the matter of the *get,* the right to culture should be approached from the perspective of women's cultural rights. A human rights based solution should explore the issue to understand the customs involved. Additionally, it should take into account the types of support women within the culture would find useful. Activists, religious leaders, legislators, and judges have participated in the attempts to solve this problem. The New York example shows that issues of gender and religion do not have simple solutions, especially from the state, which cannot fully solve the issue. Any attempt to do so would involve the regulation of religion. The ultimate solution will come from within the group, but the state can have a role as long as it does not attempt to interfere. The balancing of individual women's rights and the rights of a religious community are difficult, but success is more likely when the perspective of the religious women is taken into account.

The *get* presents a complicated problem for women. However, in contrast to scholars suggesting the exit option for members of a minority facing discriminatory policies, a closer look at this controversy shows that women are not seeking exit. An exit is possible. For the *agunot,* they are citizens of the larger state and freely able to marry in the eyes of the state. Reform Judaism does not require a *get.* The availability of an *exit* is not why women have sought help in the legislatures and the judiciary. Women want the right to *remain.* As a look at the proposed solutions suggests, this is complicated, possibly more so than the right of exit. The concept of exit is one in which a person makes a choice to leave the group for another. The idea of using the larger society as leverage to create change within the minority is implicit in Shachar's approach. However, the assumption is that women will opt out if they are continued to be treated unfairly or that the state will intervene into the substance of a religious or cultural practice. What is unaccounted for is the situation in which the state avoids delving into the substance of a religious or cultural practice, like the reluctance of judges regarding the *get,* or in which women spend years attempting to receive a *get.*

This is a multilayered and longstanding problem, and a complete solution from the state or religion may be expected soon. Women are tackling this issue on multiple fronts from within the community, through asking religious leaders to address the issue and picketing recalcitrant husbands, and outside through the legislature and judiciary. The New York laws, although there has been some criticism, have not caused constitutional problems nor problems of validity within the community. However, the ultimate solution will not come from the state. These are only partial solutions, which women have looked to for support, as they lobby for change within the community that they do not want to feel forced to leave.

4

A MOTHER'S RIGHT TO CHOOSE HER CHILDREN'S CULTURE: *MISSISSIPPI BAND OF CHOCTAW INDIANS V. HOLYFIELD*

In the previous chapter I examined the issue of the *get* and showed that the exit option does not fully address the relationship between gender and culture. Women should not have to choose between the protection of gender rights and cultural or religious identity. Women may want to remain within the group and may seek help from the larger society in achieving this end. *Mississippi Band of Choctaw Indians v. Holyfield* further complicates the concept of exit. It is the story of a tug-of-war between the Choctaw people and a non-Indian adoptive family over two young children. While the parties involved are the tribe, the adoptive parents, and the children, at the heart of this case is a question of the definition of cultural identity and group membership, as well as a tension between individual choice and community concerns. Other investigations of this and similar cases resulting from the Indian Child Welfare Act have focused on issues of jurisdiction and the "best interests of the child" in deciding child placement. However, this analysis ignores the underlying competing human rights claims that shape this conflict: gender versus culture.

Cultural theorists and rights scholars have long debated the meaning, and sometimes even the existence, of group identity and group rights. Many Western feminists advocate individualism and view an emphasis on cultural rights as detrimental to the cause of gender equality. A focus on the rights of individuals within a group often centers upon the individual's right to exit. However, the right of exit and the rights of individuals versus the group, as well as the rights of women versus culture, are most complicated in the case of a child's cultural identity. At first, this case may appear to support an argument that gender and culture are at odds. However, a closer examination can reveal a much more complicated picture of the intricate relationship between women, children and culture. This case also calls into question several assumptions about the nature of exit and the definition of culture.

Background of the *Holyfield* Case

Mississippi Band of Choctaw Indians v. Holyfield reached the United States Supreme Court in 1989 after a protracted court battle. The saga began on December 29, 1985 in the town of Gulfport, Mississippi, located in Harrison County, when Jennie Bell gave birth to twins and put them up for adoption.[201] Both parents were unmarried and both were members of the Choctaw Indian tribe, residing on a reservation located in central Mississippi's Neshoba County, approximately 200 miles from Gulfport. They both consented to give up the children for adoption.[202] Orrey Curtiss Holyfield and Vivian Joan Holyfield filed for adoption of the twins and the decree of adoption was issued in Harrison County on January 28, 1986, when the children were nearly one month old.[203] Orrey Holyfield was sixty years old at the time, and his wife forty-five. While Mr. Holyfield had six children from a previous marriage, he and Vivian Holyfield had no children together. The Holyfields paid for all of Bell's and the children's substantial medical bills incurred because the children were born two months premature.[204] Jennie Bell and the children's father voluntarily placed the twins with the Holyfields and arranged to give birth to the children off the reservation.

The Choctaw filed a motion to vacate the adoption decree two months later. They claimed the Harrison County court did not have the proper authority to issue an adoption decree in this case because exclusive jurisdiction belonged to the tribal court under the provisions of the Indian Child Welfare Act of 1978.[205] ICWA, as the act is known, states that tribes have exclusive jurisdiction over the placement of Indian children residing on Indian lands. It further requires the state to transfer jurisdiction to tribal court in cases involving Indian children not living on tribal lands at the request of the parent, guardian, or the tribe unless the parent objects, the tribe fails to file for jurisdiction, or the state can show cause.[206] The court held that the tribe did not have jurisdiction because the birth mother

---

[201] *In the Matter of B.B. and G.B., Minors; Mississippi Band of Choctaw Indians v. Holyfield* (1987). 511 So. 2d, p. 919.

[202] Richard B. Taylor (1991). "Curbing the Erosion of Rights of Native Americans: Was the Supreme Court Successful in *Mississippi Band of Choctaw Indians v. Holyfield?*" *Journal of Family Law*, 29(1): 172.

[203] Supra n201.

[204] "High Court to Weigh Custody of Twins." *The New York Times*, June 2, 1988: C13.

[205] Diane Allbaugh (1991). "Tribal Jurisdiction over Indian Children: *Mississippi Band of Choctaw Indians v. Holyfield." American Indian Law Review*, 16(2): 554.

[206] Ibid., pp. 538-539.

had made sure the children were born off the reservation, and therefore they were never residents of the reservation.[207] Further, the court took into account the voluntary nature of the placement. Both birth parents had agreed to give the children up for adoption to the Holyfields. The birth parents consented to the adoption in January of 1986 and reaffirmed their commitment to it in affidavits filed for the lower court hearing of the tribe's case.[208] The birth parents clearly intended to give their children to the Holyfields, who paid all the hospital bills, and Jennie Bell went to great lengths to give birth far from the tribal lands, thus avoiding ICWA, or so she thought.

The Choctaw appealed their case to the Mississippi Supreme Court in 1987, which concurred with the lower court's ruling. The main question in the case was the residence of the children because that determined the applicability of ICWA. Although the tribe argued the children were domiciled on the reservation during the biological mother's pregnancy, the court ultimately rejected that argument, stating that "[t]he domicile of B.B. and G.B has been and continues to be Harrison County[.]"[209] The state Supreme Court feared the tribe's residency argument would set a dangerous precedent were the court to embrace it, but the court took a very narrow reading of the statute in regards to "domicile."[210] The State of Mississippi found that ICWA did not apply in the *Holyfield* case. The twins were now nearly two years old and had continuously resided with Orrey and Vivian Holyfield, but this was not the end of the court battle.

The Choctaw appealed the ruling to the United States Supreme Court. Justice William Brennan handed down the Court's opinion in April 1989. The Court ruled in favor of the Choctaw, stating that they have exclusive jurisdiction in this adoption proceeding. Unlike the state court, the U.S. Supreme Court applied a broader reading of ICWA and attempted to discern the legislative intent. ICWA's purpose was to give tribes the power to decide the fate of their own children and to right past wrongs of Indian child removal that had threatened the survival of many indigenous peoples in the United States.

The domicile of the child was an important part of the test of applicability of this statute; however, there was no clear definition in the act. "In the absence of a statutory definition, it is generally assumed that the legislative purpose is expressed by the ordinary meaning of the words

---

[207] Supra n202, p. 173.

[208] Supra n201, p. 920.

[209] Ibid.

[210] Ibid.

used[.] Well-settled common-law principles provide that the domicile of minors ... is determined by that of their parents[.]"[211] In the case of unmarried parents, the residence of the mother is used and Jennie Bell was a resident of the reservation. The twins were domiciled on the reservation, even though they had never been there. The Court also noted that voluntary placement with an adoptive family did not change their primary residence or the jurisdiction of their custody case.[212]

The Choctaw won in a landmark case upholding ICWA. The Court vacated the adoption and returned the matter to the tribal court. It was apparently a victory for cultural rights and self-determination, but the tribal court had not yet ruled and the "best interests of the children" were not resolved. The twins were two and a half years old.

During the Supreme Court proceedings, Orrey Holyfield died, but Vivian Holyfield continued to fight for custody. The case was remanded to the tribal court where it took some surprising twists. The biological father had given his consent to the adoption in January of 1986, prior to the adoption by the Holyfields. This was an important part of the adoption process because it ensured that both parents were giving informed consent to the termination of their parental rights. It had always added to the Holyfields' case that neither parent wanted to raise the child as a Choctaw. However, the Choctaw tribal court found the alleged biological father was not the actual biological father of the twins. His consent was meaningless. Equally surprising was the court's final ruling. In the end, the tribal court ruled that the children's interests would be served best by remaining with Vivian Holyfield, but they would maintain contact with the tribe and the children's biological extended family.[213] Even though the tribal court won the right to decide the children's fate, its decision kept the children with the non-Indian parent, Vivian Holyfield. However, the tribal court created a middle ground by mandating contact for the twins with their extended biological families and the tribe as a whole.

---

[211] *Mississippi Band of Choctaw Indians v. Holyfield* (1989). 490 U.S. 30, 109 S. Ct. 1597, 104 L. Ed. 2d 31.

[212] Supra n208.

[213] Supra n205, p. 558. Referenced from *Holyfield v. Choctaw Social Services/Mississippi Band of Choctaw Indians, The Natural Mother and Alleged Natural Father*, No. AD 017-90. (Mississippi Band of Choctaw Indians Tribal Court, July 27, 1990, recorded in Adoption Book A, pp. 89-90. See also Senate Indian Affairs and House Resources Comittees (June 18, 1997). Testimony of Thomas L. Leclaire, Director of the Office of Tribal Justice, Department of Justice. Available at page 3 of www.senate.gov/~scia/hearings/818_doj.htm.

The Significance of the *Holyfield Decision*

Given this final outcome, it is hard to tell which side actually won in this case. The Supreme Court upheld ICWA stating that tribes should determine the placement of their children, but the twins remained with the non-Indian adoptive parent. The children would be raised between two cultures. Is this outcome what Congress intended when it passed ICWA? What are the best interests of the child? The biological mother attempted to circumvent ICWA and, in the end, she was mostly successful. However, the Supreme Court decision makes it doubtful the outcome of this case is more than an aberration. This case begs the question: what are women's rights in the matter of choosing their children's identities?

The scholarship on *Holyfield* is thin. For most authors writing on ICWA, this case is practically a footnote, even though it is the only case on this subject to reach the United States Supreme Court. Diane Allbaugh's article from *American Indian Law Review* examines this case as an example of "the Court tackl[ing] the difficult task of balancing the interests of the tribe, the child, and the state."[214] She sees *Holyfield* in the context of federalism and family law, a problem of wide-ranging state court decisions and maintaining Indian families. Her solution is greater scrutiny from the federal judiciary and clarified federal ICWA guidelines from the Congress. Basically, the government should further legislate tribes and state courts in order to give tribes more sovereignty. The premise of her article is that tribes will always do what is in the best interest of the children because they know that the best interests lie in maintaining the Indian family. However, the outcome of *Holyfield* does not support that claim. Furthermore, the maintenance of Indian families appears to be based upon involuntary removal of children. *Holyfield* concerns a voluntary placement and the suggestion that government regulate further Indian identity proceedings appears to fly in the face of the goal of self-determination.

Richard Taylor's article, entitled "Curbing the Erosion of the Rights of Native Americans," also focuses on the issue of jurisdiction stemming from federal law and divergent judicial systems and political goals. Taylor advocates greater involvement from the federal judiciary in order to monitor state court actions.[215] Neither article addresses the problem I assert is central to this case: does a mother have the right to exit for her child?

---

[214] Supra n205, p. 557.

[215] Supra n202, p. 188.

The Justifications for the Indian Child Welfare Act

Before the passage of ICWA, Indian families had been decimated under the guise of the protection of children. Marilyn Holt's *Indian Orphanages* traces the history of Indian adoption, foster care, and orphanages in the United States. The numbers of the indigenous persons in North America was drastically reduced following contact with Europeans. Disease and ecological warfare threatened native peoples. For example, tribes such as the Comanche, Pawnee, and Catawbas lost half of their respective populations to smallpox epidemics in the eighteenth and early nineteenth centuries. Destruction of food sources such as the buffalo in the West and the relocation of entire peoples to lands less desired by Europeans also contributed to the circumstances of the indigenous peoples.[216] In the nineteenth and twentieth centuries, education and assimilation have been the tools for the cultural genocide of American Indians.

Holt's work offers in-depth case studies of Indian residential schools and orphanages over the past two hundred years. She moves between Quaker schools in upstate New York to orphanages in North Dakota, illustrating the dual threads of cultural destruction and survival that run through this history. Missionary groups ran many residential schools and saw themselves as saviors of the tribes by teaching Christianity, as well as English, in order to enculturate Indian children.

While U.S. government institutions had some of the same goals as Indian orphanages that were set up throughout the nation, these facilities were also located on tribal lands and still gave Indian children access to their cultures.[217] She asserts that the closure of these facilities in favor of off-reservation boarding schools or merely local American schools created the real cultural genocide still evident today.[218] Children were removed from their communities for their own good, but were denied knowledge of their identities and were forced to become part of the European-American dominated society.

The removal of children from their communities because one or both parents had died, or for other reasons such as abuse, neglect, or abandonment, became a noticeable crisis to mainstream society by the 1970s. Lorie Graham writes that "one-third of all Native American children were being separated from their families and communities and placed in non-Indian adoptive homes, foster care, educational institutions by federal, state and

---

[216] Marilyn Irvin Holt (2001). *Indian Orphanages*. Lawrence, KS: University Press of Kansas, pp. 38-39.

[217] Ibid., p. 257.

[218] Ibid., p. 258.

private child welfare authorities" before the enactment of ICWA.[219] The high-rate of removal of children from Indian homes was brought out in 1974–1977 Congressional hearings, in which Congress found the displacement of children to be due to a lack of understanding of Indian culture and a "bias against Indian culture in state courts and welfare agencies."[220] In response, the legislature passed *The Indian Child Welfare Act of 1978*. It gave tribal courts jurisdiction over the custody of children and sought to mend the wounds of generations of forced exile from indigenous culture. Along with the previously mentioned provisions of ICWA is the mandate that in the case of adoption, the child should be offered to first to the extended family, then the tribe, and, lastly, another Indian family.[221] This aspect of ICWA is meant to ensure indigenous children remain in their cultures. ICWA, in general, promotes tribal sovereignty, culture, and the maintenance of kinship ties not found outside of the group. ICWA is meant as a tool for indigenous survival in a nation-state premised on individual rights and cultural assimilation.

The situation in which children were placed with non-Indian families may have persisted because the government failed to understand the cultural values of Indian peoples and felt that "a non-Indian household [could] only benefit an Indian child."[222] The passage of ICWA has not changed this situation because lawyers, judges, and parents often circumvent the provisions of the law. Also, the definition of family in the act reflects the family values of the dominant American society and does not allow for the types of living arrangements that might be made within the tribe.[223] In short, American notions of family leave out community. Carole Goldberg-Ambrose's "Heeding the 'Voice' of Tribal Law in Indian Child Welfare Proceedings" also touches on this point. Her article seeks to illustrate the state court bias against Indian children and tribes by showing the different, and much larger, conception of families in tribes and enumerates how application of this would transform Indian child welfare proceedings.[224] She uses critical race theory to examine ICWA and finds

---

[219] Lorie M. Graham (1998). "'The Past Never Vanishes': A Contextual Critique of the Existing Indian Family Doctrine." *American Indian Law Review*, 23(1): 2.

[220] David Null (1985). "The Indian Child Welfare Act." *Journal of Juvenile Law*, 9(2): 391.

[221] Supra n211, p. 37.

[222] Supra n219.

[223] Ibid., p. 4.

[224] Carole Goldberg-Ambrose (1994). "Heeding the 'Voice' of Tribal Law in Indian Child Welfare Proceedings." In René Kuppe and Richard Potz (Eds.) (1994). *Law and Anthropology: International Yearbook for Legal Anthropology*, vol. 7. Dordrecht; Boston; London: Martinus Nijhoff Publishers, p. 4.

that the bias in state courts manifests itself mainly through the argument of "the best interests of the children."[225]

Indian children are thus subject to two distinct and overlapping legal systems. This conflict is apparent in cases of adoption in which the adoptive parents are non-Indian or in custody battles in which a parent is non-Indian. Goldberg-Ambrose argues that in these cases, state courts are more likely to side with the non-Indians citing the best interests of the child.[226] However, Jeanne Louise Carriere contends that the problem of state court bias exists because tribes are forced to allow state courts to decide many Indian adoptions due to the "good cause" provision in ICWA.[227] This aspect of the law allows states to maintain jurisdiction over adoptions and other custody decisions involving Indian children, if they can prove why the cases do not belong in tribal court. In *Holyfield*, the Mississippi trial court used the twins' birth in Gulfport as the primary reason to maintain jurisdiction. Carriere finds the act unsuccessful because "[t]he purpose of the ICWA is to ameliorate the problems of unnecessary interventions into Native American families[;]" however, the "good cause" provision creates further state intervention because state courts will not give up jurisdiction willingly.[228] The bias against tribes prompts judges to examine cases in such a way as to use the "good cause" argument to keep Indian children away from their own traditional justice systems, and to impose a foreign one that represents their best interests by denying them access to their cultures.

These authors all challenge ICWA on the basis of group rights versus individual rights and federalism. They paint state courts as zealous individualists and assimilationists, and they paint tribes, as well as the federal government, oddly enough, as champions of cultural rights. Still, the federal government's commitment has limits. ICWA is Congress's first attempt at returning custody jurisdiction to tribes, and it falls short of full self-determination. Neither has Congress barred the state from adjudicating all Indian custody cases, which these authors suggest is vital to the autonomy and survival of native peoples.

---

[225] Ibid., p. 21.

[226] Ibid.

[227] Jeanne Louise Carriere (1994). "Representing the Native American: Culture, Jurisdiction, and the Indian Child Welfare Act." *Iowa Law Review*, 79(3): 646-647.

[228] Ibid.

Related Cases and Transracial Adoption

Barring state courts from custody cases involving all Indian children in order to maintain indigenous communities assumes the children in question retain a singular, immutable cultural identity that could be recognized through legal autonomy in these types of family law proceedings. While *Mississippi Band of Choctaw Indians v. Holyfield* is the only ICWA case to reach the Supreme Court, there are an incredible number of ICWA cases, so this means continually putting the 1978 Act to the test and further complicating the assumptions of children's cultural identity. For example, *In re Wanomi P.* states that ICWA did not apply in that case, because the biological mother was a member of a Canadian tribe, not a U.S. tribe.[229] Much of the literature on Indian adoptions assumes the birth parents to be part of the same indigenous community, but this case illustrates the definitions embedded in the notion of indigenous status, because it is only available to those whose people reside within the country's boundaries. The true meaning of indigenous is a people inhabiting lands before modern nation-state boundaries, and existing as citizens of both tribes and states, and sometimes neither.

The most contentious and problematic Indian adoption cases involve a non-Indian parent and an Indian parent. In *Morrow v. Winslow*, biological parents chose to give up their newborn child to a couple specified as The Does in the court papers. The birth father subsequently challenged the adoption. He was a member of the Cherokee nation. Although he had originally agreed, he now sought custody of the child under ICWA and made a motion for the case to be moved to tribal court.[230] The birth mother, Carol Grant, objected. She wanted the child, Creedence, to be adopted, and feared her wishes would not be carried out if the case were transferred to the tribal court. Morrow's motion was denied and the state court ruled that his consent was actually unnecessary for the adoption.[231] In this case, ICWA appears ill-equipped. The birth mother was not a member of a tribe. She wanted to place her child up for adoption and did not want the child's father or his family to have contact with the child. She objected to moving the case to the tribal court, fearing her interests would not be represented there. This appears to be a position unaccounted for in ICWA. Most of the ICWA scholars would agree that the tribe should have had jurisdiction in this case, even if that position limits the rights of the birth mother.

---

[229] *In re Wanomi P.*, 216 Cal. App. 3d 156, 264 Cal.Rptr. 623 (1989).

[230] *Morrow v. Winslow*, 94 F.3d 1386 (10th Cir. 1996).

[231] Ibid.

The child can be said to have claim to *both* identities, and placement of the child becomes a greater conundrum when the choice is between a non-Indian adoptive couple and the tribe for these children. *In re Bridget R.* was a 1996 case from California. Although the birth mother was a non-Indian, the birth father was eligible to be a member of the Pomo Indian tribe. Both sought to give the twins, Bridget and Lucy, up for adoption. The birth father chose not to disclose his Indian heritage, fearing it would slow the adoption.[236] They chose the Rosts from Ohio as the adoptive parents. They had no plans for any involvement of their families in the lives of the twin girls.[237] The paternal grandparents of the children convinced the birth parents to file a claim under ICWA because the father was eligible for tribal membership. Joan Heifetz Hollinger questions ICWA because it defines as only Indian, children with a diverse heritage, thus denying them access to their cultural heritage.[238]

Like the *Morrow* case, *In re Bridget R.* questions the fairness of ICWA for the non-Indian birth parent and the child. Under ICWA, there can be no voluntary placements and there is no room for biculturalism. One is either a tribal member and under the tribe's jurisdiction or one is part of the nation-state and subject to the jurisdiction of the state. These cases also have in common the interests of the extended families. Neither father in these cases petitions for custody only because he wants it. His parents are large figures in both cases. They appear, especially in *Bridget R.*, to be pushing for the children's return to the family even though the birth parents had made the decision to give them up outside of the tribe.

This family interest in the children shows that ICWA cases are not always purely about a birth mother's desire to have her child adopted off the reservation versus cultural respect and autonomy. Through the Indian Child Welfare Act, members of the extended family can assert their rights to maintain kinship ties. U.S. family law requires the consent of only the birth mother and father, although the father's consent was added later. Family law is tainted with the omnipresence of individual autonomy. Only the parents need consent, but the extended family is also losing a member, and they have no voice in these proceedings. ICWA has given Indian families a way to counteract the loss of children from the tribe. However, not all parents wish for grandparents to have a say in decisions involving

---

[236] *In re Bridget R.*, 41 Cal App. 4th 1483, 49 Cal.Rptr.2d 507 (1996), *cert. denied*, 519 U.S. 1060 (1997).

[237] Joan Heifetz Hollinger (1996), "Children of the Tribe—Determining Children's Identity under the Indian Child Welfare Act," *U.C.-Davis Journal of of Juvenile Law and Policy.* 1: 19-23 (comment on *Bridget R*, 41 Cal. App. 4th, 49 Cal. Rptr. 2d 507, examining factual context).

[238] Supra n233.

children. Eric Andersen contends that non-parents are increasingly seeking "legally enforceable relationships with [a] child against the wishes of the parent."[235] And, courts are becoming more likely to grant those requests as being within the best interests of the child. This is not to say that non-parents are now winning custody over parents, but the rights of those other than the parents to have access to the child are more commonly recognized. In the case of the tribe, they are especially important because the extended family represents the child's tie to the community and the culture. To sever that bond would be more than the loss of a family member, it would be to weaken the cultural community as a whole.

In addition to the controversy over the placement of Indian children, there has been a substantial amount of scholarly work written regarding transracial adoption that is applicable to these cases. In examining this debate, Twila Perry notes early on that the number of transracial adoptions and biracial children is small. Her focus is on African-American children, and she finds the debate to be too focused on the margins of society. She feels that transracial adoptions are too rare to warrant the attention they are getting. However, she still finds fault with the purveyors of the attitude that colorblind adoption is best,because these scholars seem to assume adoptions can work only one way—non-white child with white parents.[236] This assumption is paternalistic and racist. It forces children to bear the brunt of adapting to a background different from their natural environment. It paints white adoptive couples as the saviors of the poor children of color.

Perry's argument supports ICWA as an attempt to place children within their own cultures, such as in the *Holyfield* case, but identity is not the clear-cut issue Perry and the supporters of ICWA would have one believe. *Morrow* and *Bridget R.* are both cases in which one parent is a non-Indian. Do the non-Indian parents, both mothers in these cases, have the right to pass along an identity and reject the tribe? Perry would argue that the children would still be defined as Indian in the white culture, so birth mothers are doing their children no favor by placing them in white homes. They will always be Indian to non-Indians, but is that enough to justify

---

[235] Eric G. Andersen (1998). "Children, Parents, and Non-parents: Protected Interests and Legal Standards." *Brigham Young University Law Review*, 1998: 935.

[236] Twila L. Perry (1993-1994). "The Transracial Adoption Controversy: An Analysis of Discourse and Subordination." *New York University Review of Law and Social Change*, 21(1): 106. Compare, for a counter-perspective, Joan Heifetz Hollinger (1996), "The Uniform Adoption Act," *Family Law Quarterly*, 30(2): 345-378; and Joan Heifetz Hollinger (1995), "Revisiting the Issues: The Uniform Adoption Act," *Future of Children*, 5(3): 205-211.

ICWA and denying birth mothers their rights to choose their children's homes in the name of culture?

Gender vs. Culture: The Right of Exit

Holyfield, like *Morrow* and *Bridget R.*, is a case in which the tribe sought to go against the wishes of the birth mother. Jennie Bell chose to place her children with Vivian Holyfield. Although sidelined in the case in which Vivian Holyfield argued for the best interests of the children, Bell maintained her will to have the children adopted. She chose for her children to exit the Choctaw culture, but there are several human rights implications for such a choice. *The International Covenant on Economic, Social, and Cultural Rights*, Article 15 states that everyone has the right "to take part in cultural life."[237] However, the *International Covenant on Civil Political Rights* makes a stronger statement in Article 27:

> In those states in which ethnic, religious, or linguistic minorities exist, persons belonging to such minorities shall not be denied the right, in community with other members of their group, to enjoy their own culture, to profess and practise their own religion, or to use their own language.[238]

International human rights treaties have codified the right to culture, but the gender component to this right is not addressed in any of the human rights treaties. The Women's Convention, created in the 1970s, attacks states for promoting stereotypes of women and discrimination against them.[239] A woman's right to exit a culture for her child is not addressed at all. The closest would be Article 16, which relates to marriage and family. However, it does not mention the issue of adoption.

The convention that most closely relates to the issues of gender, culture, and adoption is the *Convention on the Rights of the Child*, which entered into force in 1990. The purpose of this Convention is to protect children from both the state and their parents.[240] It includes provisions relating to adoption in Articles 5-9 and Articles 21-22. The most relevant is Article 8.1, which mandates that: "state parties undertake to respect the right of the child to preserve her or her identity, including nationality,

---

[237] United Nations (1966). *International Covenant on Economic, Social, and Cultural Rights*, Article 15(a). Entered into force on January 3, 1976.

[238] United Nations (1966). *International Covenant on Civil and Political Rights*, Article 27. Entered into force on March 23, 1979.

[239] See United Nations (1979). *Convention on the Elimination of All Forms of Discrimination against Women*, Article 5. Entered into force on September 3, 1981.

[240] United Nations (1989). *Convention on the Rights of the Child*. Adopted by the General Assembly November 20, 1989. Entered into force on September 2, 1990.

name and family relations as recognised by law without unlawful interference," and Article 30, which specifies a right to culture like that of Article 27 of the *International Covenant on Civil and Political Rights*.[241] While these Articles appear to support ICWA, they make no mention of the issue: at what point a child is considered to possess a cultural identity. Article 30 states that children "belonging to" minorities are entitled to be a part of that culture.[242] It assumes the child's identity will follow that of the birth parents. However, this is not necessarily the case in trans-cultural adoption or when parents have chosen to exit their cultural communities.

Although no treaty specifically governs this case, it is again important to return to the Human Rights Committee's decision in the case of Sandra Lovelace, which addressed a woman's right to her culture as well as to her choice to leave it. *Lovelace v. Canada* is the most obvious example of a human rights conflict between gender and culture. However, it did not really touch on the right of exit for one's child. Chandran Kukathas and Will Kymlicka have written extensively on cultural rights. Kymlicka contends that both group rights and individual rights can coexist. Kukathas, on the other hand, sees groups as merely a collection of individuals possessing no special collective rights. Kukuthas's fixation on the right to exit the group grows from this individual rights premise.[243] To embrace group rights, he would have to allow for limitations on the rights of individuals. The right of exit is an important feature of his thought because it gives the individual the freedom to choose to opt out of an oppressive culture.

Susan Moller Okin and Ayelet Shachar would agree. They both add a gender component to multicultural theory and question the relationship between gender and culture. Susan Moller Okin's 1999 book *Is Multiculturalism Bad for Women?* examines this issue and asserts that an emphasis on cultural accommodations would be detrimental to women because "they treat cultures as monoliths ... [ignoring that they] are themselves *gendered,* with substantial differences in power and advantage between

---

[241] Ibid., Article 8; supra n238, Article 27.

[242] Article 27 (supra n.238) states that "[i]n those States in which ethnic, religious or linguistic minorities or persons of indigenous origin exist, a child belonging to such a minority or who is indigenous shall not be denied the right, in community with other members of his or her group, to enjoy his or her own culture, to profess and practise his or her own religion, or to use his or her own language."

[243] Chandran Kukathas (1992). "Are There any Cultural Rights?" *Political Theory*, 20(1): 105-139. See also Chandran Kukathas (1997). "Cultural Toleration." In Ian Shapiro and Will Kymlicka (Eds.) (1997). *Ethnicity and Group Rights.* New York; London: New York University Press, pp. 69-104; Will Kymlicka (1995). *Multicultural Citizenship: A Liberal Theory of Minority Rights.* Oxford: Clarendon Press.

men and women."[244] Although Ayelet Shachar's 2001 book *Multicultural Jurisdictions*[245] contains a more thoughtful version of the argument, both theorists come to the conclusion that women's rights will be violated by cultural accommodations because culture has been defined in male terms. Shachar worries that a focus on limiting only the "external restrictions" on groups will not solve problems of inequality within group rules. Okin takes a more absolutist position on this point, but Shachar argues for a layering of jurisdiction that would avoid the "all or nothing" cultural accommodations feminist scholars often fear.[246] Culture is always against women, but the cultures they examine are minority cultures. They do not reference the impact of their own cultures on their lives.

Complicating the Relationship between Gender and Culture

Do women have a right to choose cultural identity for their children that is different from their own? This is the main issue in *Holyfield*, and it is the question scholars have left unanswered. To believe in the right to culture and to also believe in the rights of women is not to adhere to two mutually exclusive systems of belief. Culture and gender may appear to collide, but they also coexist. Women assert their rights to culture, and they also assert their rights to leave their cultures or to allow their children to do so. The right to exit has been theorized in male terms. To reconceptualize it to include women would necessitate including children. This does not bestow upon women any special rights. Women, and parents in general, have always chosen the culture of their children. In the cases of Bridget and Lucy R. and Creedence Morrow, they are caught between cultures, and it is obvious that decisions regarding their upbringing will shape their cultural identity. However, more subtle decisions such as living near or far from relatives are made every day by parents and guardians in the majority culture. When Jennie Bell gave her twins to Vivian Holyfield, she was exercising her autonomy as an individual and her right as a mother to decide the identity of the children.

The Indian Child Welfare Act represents an attempt to protect the indigenous peoples of the United States, but as *Holyfield* and related cases have shown, its execution has been paternalistic and male-biased. The Act does not permit women such as Jennie Bell to make a voluntary decision to

---

[244] Susan Moller Okin (1999). *Is Multiculturalism Bad for Women?* Princeton, NJ: Princeton University Press, p. 12.

[245] Ayelet Shachar (2001). *Multicultural Jurisdictions*. Cambridge: Cambridge University Press.

[246] Ibid., p. 126.

place her child outside of the tribe. The tribe and the federal government professed to know what was best. Taking away women's agency in matters of children appears to be a slippery slope toward full regulation of women's bodies on tribal lands. For instance, could a tribe enjoin a woman from having an abortion because the extended Indian family and community have an interest in promoting births? This may seem to be a far-fetched example, but it is not too far removed from the paternalistic way in which the ICWA is adjudicated.

The tribal court, the state court, the U.S. Supreme Court, and Congress have all shaped the Act that defined where and by whom Indian children may be raised. However, every one of those institutions is male-dominated. They define culture so that men are the models of individuals. Policies and provisions do not take the needs of women into account. Denying women the choice of voluntary placement of children without tribal approval robs them of their choices and of their individuality.

When women choose for their children to exit the culture, they are making a statement. They are choosing for their children what it is too late to choose for themselves—a different culture, a different life. This may be repugnant to some because women are choosing to commit cultural genocide, but the alternative is to deny women their rights as individuals to make choices concerning themselves and their bodies. Individual choice cannot exist only when it adheres to group goals.

The United States Supreme Court erred in *Mississippi Band of Choctaw Indians v. Holyfield,* and Congress erred in the passage of the Indian Child Welfare Act. These acts deny voluntary placement, thereby denying women their equal rights as tribal members and U.S. citizens. Women are set up as second-class members because they lack the legal capacity to make choices for their children's lives that conflict with tribal interests, unless they circumvent the law as Jennie Bell attempted to do. Due to this situation, it appears at first glance that women face a dilemma in which women's individual rights are at odds with the right to culture.

Nevertheless, this case lends itself to an alternate interpretation when viewed through the lens of gendered cultural rights. Examining women's right to culture in this case is to see the relationship between gender and culture and the complex interplay between the rights. Women face obstacles in invoking their right to be part of a culture due to the way men within the culture and in the larger society have defined culture. The law does not adequately take women's interests into account as members of the community. In order to protect the future of a cultural community and redress past harms, the law is overbroad. It also assumes that women and children should share the same culture and, that if women choose to relinquish custody of their children, they would not want the child to have a different identity from their own. An assumption of this debate is that for a woman to wish her child to not be raised within her culture, she too must reject the culture. This case shows that the relationship between women, children, and culture is much more complicated. Gender and culture are not at odds, only male-dominated and male-defined culture. Cultural survival is important, but not at the expense of women's freedom.

5

CONCEPTUALIZING THE RIGHT OF WOMEN TO THEIR OWN CULTURE: THE HINDMARSH ISLAND BRIDGE AFFAIR

The Hindmarsh Island Bridge Affair is the final case I will examine. Although the bridge at the center of the dispute has now been completed, this case holds a place of importance in the field of human rights. It presents a different set of issues for women's cultural rights. Unlike the other controversies analyzed in previous chapters, such as the Headscarf debate in France, this is not a case in which women argue as individuals for a greater gendered cultural identity. The Hindmarsh case affords insight into women's collective right to culture and the ensuing challenges such a formulation poses for theorizing about human rights.

The history of the Hindmarsh Island Bridge Affair is long and complex, involving both legislative and judicial remedies, as well as obstacles for a claim of a gendered cultural right. The subject of Hindmarsh Island, called the secret "women's business," was debated in the mainstream majority culture of Australia. At the crux of this dispute have been the rights of indigenous people, cultural rights and heritage, the politics of authenticity, the identity of the proper representative of the group, state and federal politics, and mechanisms for adjudication. These issues complicated the attempt invoke women's right to culture. In contrast to the cases in the previous chapters, women are, from the beginning, framing their argument as one of cultural rights specific to women. However, the collective nature of a group rights claim by only one gender within a community appears to pose the largest obstacle to the success of the human rights claim. The Hindmarsh Island Bridge Affair illustrates the difficulty of invoking a gendered cultural rights claim through an existing mechanism when this concept is absent from human rights theory and law.

History of the Hindmarsh Island Bridge Affair

Hindmarsh Island, also known as Kumarangk to the Aborigines of the area, is located in the state of South Australia in Lake Alexandrina.[247] The Chapmans, owners of Binalong Pty Ltd, purchased land on Hindmarsh Island and sought to develop a marina that included residential areas as well as businesses.[248] The only transportation between the island and the town of Goolwa was a cable-drawn ferry. Therefore, for the proposed development to take place, a bridge would have to be built.[249] An agreement with the South Australia government stipulated that Binalong would build the bridge; the government would own it as well as reimbursing the company for whichever was the lesser sum of half the cost of the bridge or three million dollars.[250] The local government hoped the development would increase tourism to the area.[251]

The project was contingent upon the building of the bridge, and the bridge construction was contingent upon Binalong completing an Environmental Impact Statement (EIS) regarding the effects of the construction.[252] During the course of compiling this report, two Aboriginal sites were discovered in the area of the proposed bridge. The anthropologist Rod Lucas, hired to consult with the Ngarrindjeri people, reported on the effects of the development alone and not the bridge. His report concluded that Hindmarsh Island would most likely be the center of a political debate over Aboriginal rights as a symbol of Aboriginal heritage and the future of that culture. He emphasized that the contemporary value of that site was as important as its past significance.[253]

By 1993, the bridge still had not been built due to financial constraints on the part of the builders and the state government. Many people believed the projects were permanently tabled.[254] Bridge construction finally began that October amid protests from local residents; it was halted on the second day of work after members of the Lower Murray Aboriginal Heritage Committee informed the State Minister for Aboriginal Affairs that the

---

[247] *Chapman and Others v. Minister for Aboriginal and Torres Strait Islander Affairs and Others; Barton and Another v. Minister for Aboriginal and Torres Strait Islander Affairs and Others.* 133 ALR 74, 79.

[248] Maureen Tehan (1996). "A Tale of Two Cultures." *Alternative Law Journal*, 21(1): 10.

[249] Ibid.

[250] Ryan, Lyndall (1996). "Origins of a Royal Commission." *Journal of Australian Studies*, 48: 3.This article comes from a special issue of *The Journal of Australian Studies* that deals entirely with the Hindmarsh Affair and "women's business." Some of the articles in this issue are cited in this paper, and all are listed in the bibliography.

[251] Ibid., p. 2.

[252] Supra n247, p. 80.

[253] Supra n250, p. 3.

[254] Ibid., p. 4.

construction had exposed burial sites.[255] The Aboriginal Legal Rights Movement (ALRM) filed complaints with both the state and federal Ministers of Aboriginal Affairs regarding the construction of the bridge.[256]

The newly elected state government commissioned a report in the early part of 1994 to assess its obligations regarding the currently halted bridge project. The conclusion of the report was that the state government had an obligation to uphold its commitments and that failure to do so would result in compensation claims from the builders possibly totaling twenty million dollars.[257] Following this, the state government authorized the construction of the bridge, even though the Draper Report on the Aboriginal sites was not submitted until two weeks after this decision.[258] This report did find evidence of Aboriginal sites in the vicinity of the construction, but not enough to cause the state to again halt the project.[259]

In April of 1994, ALRM wrote to the Federal Minister for Aboriginal and Torres Strait Islander Affairs and asked that he make an emergency declaration under section 9 of the Commonwealth Heritage Act, which would halt construction for 30 days while the claims were investigated.[260] It was also during this time that ALRM wrote again and revealed further the nature of the Aboriginal claims that construction of a bridge would be destructive to Ngarrindjeri Culture.[261]

The Minister hired Professor Saunders to investigate the claims. Through the course of her work, she followed the procedures set forth in the Heritage Act. She placed notices in the local newspapers requesting that anyone with an interest in this matter to make representation to her.[262] Dr. Fergie, an anthropologist, provided a portion of the representations that dealt with claims of secret "women's business." The details of this "women's business" were placed in sealed envelopes with instructions that they be read by women only and attached to the report.[263] Following

---

[255] Supra n250, p. 5.

[256] Ibid., p. 6.

[257] Supra n248, p. 11.

[258] Supra n250, p. 6.

[259] Supra n248, p. 11.

[260] Supra n247, p. 81.

[261] Ibid.

[262] Ibid., p. 82.

[263] Supra n250, p. 8.

the submission of Professor Saunder's report, the Minister placed a 25-year ban on the construction of the bridge on July 9, 1994.[264]

It was at this point the court battles began. The Chapmans challenged the ban in Federal Court: it handed down a decision in February of 1995 quashing both the decisions of Professor Saunders and the Minister.[265] Judge O'Loughlin's reasoning in the case was that the basis for both Professor Saunder's and the Minister's decision that Hindmarsh Island constituted a "significant Aboriginal area[,] and that it [was] under serious and immediate threat of injury or desecration"[266] was the claim of "women's business."[267] O'Loughlin went on to state the claims of "women's business" were unknown to both Professor Saunders and the Minister when the original declaration was made and the notices placed in the newspapers. Because the public had no way of knowing exactly what the Aboriginal claims were, the Judge reasoned, they could not have known if they needed to make representations or not. The Judge found the notices inadequate and further stated that the "women's business" should not have been part of either Professor Saunders' or the Minister's decision-making unless a more specific notice had been published after the claims of "women's business" surfaced.[268] This was Judge O'Loughlin's primary reason for quashing the ban.

Another important reason was the issue of the Minister's consideration of the representations. The Minister did not read the material in the sealed envelopes. He made his decision without reading the representations of the exact nature of the "women's business" on Hindmarsh Island, because the envelopes were marked that they should be read by women only. The report was vague concerning the exact nature of the "women's business" and the only full explanation of the claims was contained in the sealed envelopes. Mrs. Kee, the Minister's assistant, read the confidential representations and advised the Minister that the contents of the sealed envelopes were consistent with the Saunders Report.[269] Judge O'Loughlin stated in his decision that he was "of the opinion that it was not a proper exercise of a power on the part of the minister to rely so heavily on the

---

[264] Supra n248, p. 11.

[265] Supra n247, p. 129.

[266] *Aboriginal and Torres Strait Islander Heritage Protection Act* (1984). Sec. 9. Available at http://scaleplus.law.gov.au/ogi-bin/topic.

[267] Supra n247, p. 127.

[268] Ibid.

[269] Ibid., p. 123.

subject of women's business, yet deny himself access to the contents of the secret envelopes."[270]

Minister Tickner, among others, appealed Justice O'Loughlin's decision, but the decision was upheld by all three Justices in May of 1995.[271] The following month, the South Australian Government appointed a Royal Commission to look into the matter of "women's business." The motivation behind this event was reported allegations of fabrication and disagreement within the Ngarrindjeri community (women claiming knowledge of the "women's business" were known as the proponent women and women claiming no knowledge of the "women's business" were known as dissident women) over the existence of the "women's business."[272] The ALRM challenged the appointment of the Royal Commission under the Racial Discrimination Act of 1975. The judges did not find that the Royal Commission's inquiry would violate the Act.[273]After months of investigation and testimony, the Commission reported in December 1995 the claims of "women's business" were fabricated. However, none of the proponent women had testified before the commission.[274]

The Royal Commission, to which ALRM and the proponent women had objected, was itself now under scrutiny. A federal inquiry was to follow the Royal Commission in deciding the validity of the proponent women's claims.[275] In January 1996 the Minister appointed a Justice from the Federal Court of Australia, Justice Jane Matthews, to write another report regarding the claims of "women's business" in the Hindmarsh Island Bridge Affair. With the appointment of a woman, this inquiry could possibly have yielded a different outcome regarding the scrutiny of the women's claims. However, the constitutionality of appointing a Federal Court Judge to prepare the report was challenged in the High Court, the court of last resort in Australia, and subsequently ruled unconstitutional.[276]

---

[270] Ibid., p. 125.

[271] *Norvill and Another v. Chapman and Others; Novill and Another v. Barton and Others; Tickner v. Chapman and Others; Tickner v. Barton and Others,* 133 ALR 226, p. 272.

[272] Supra n248, p. 11.

[273] *The Aboriginal Legal Rights Movement, Inc. v. The State of South Australia and Iris Eliza Stevens* (1995). 64 ASR 551.

[274] Garth Nettheim (1996). "Women's Business and Law." *Aboriginal Law Bulletin,* 3(80): 24.

[275] Marcia Langton (1996). "The Hindmarsh Island Bridge Affair: How Aboriginal Women's Religion Became an Administrable Affair." *Australian Feminist Studies,* 11(24): 215.

[276] *Wilson and Ors v. The Minister for Aboriginal and Torres Strait Islander Affairs and Anor.* (1996). 189 CLR 1.

In 1997 the South Australia Parliament enacted the Hindmarsh Island Bridge Act. It stated that the Heritage Protection Act did not protect Hindmarsh Island from the construction of a bridge and/or any activities relating to its construction and/or maintenance. The act also disallowed the Minister from acting on any claim relating to the Hindmarsh Island.[277] Doreen Kartinyeti, the spokesperson for the proponent women, among others, challenged this law in the High Court in 1998. Plaintiffs claimed that the Hindmarsh Island Bridge Act 1997 was unconstitutional. The court upheld the act, ruling that it did not violate the constitution nor was it in conflict with the Heritage Protection Act.[278]

Bridge construction began again on Hindmarsh Island in October 1999. The Supreme Court denied the Ngarrindjeri's request for an injunction.[279] The construction site has been the focus of constant protesting since construction resumed and until the opening of the bridge on March 4, 2001.[280] The Chapmans, owners of Binalong, who sought to develop a marina on Hindmarsh Island, filed suit in Federal Court against the former Minister Tickner, Professor Saunders, Dr. Fergie, and the Commonwealth for a sum of twenty million dollars in damages.[281] During the course of the litigation, Minister Tickner was finally forced by the court to read Dr. Fergie's report.[282] Following the opening of the bridge, the development on Hindmarsh Island has flourished and created an economic boom for the local economy.[283]

The Validity of the Claims of "Women's Business"

This case has attracted both media and academic interest. However, in all that has been written about the Hindmarsh Island Bridge Affair, the majority of it has concentrated on the central element of the debate—does secret "women's business" exist? This was the question the Royal Commission posed and the focus of the media's interest.

---

[277] South Australia Parliament (1997). *Hindmarsh Island Bridge Act*. No. 60 of 1997—Assented to 22 May 1997, Sec. 4.

[278] *Doreen Kartinyeri and Anor v. The Commonwealth of Australia* (1998). 152 ALR 540.

[279] Tim Dornin (Oct. 27, 1999). "SA: Court Rules against Fresh Bid to Stop Hindmarsh Bridge." *AAP NEWSFEED.*

[280] Sherrill Nixon (Dec. 13, 1999). "SA: Hindmarsh Island Bridge Case in Court." *AAP NEWSFEED.*

[281] Ibid.

[282] Kate Uren (Nov. 14, 2000). "Tickner Finds Out Why He Imposed Ban." *The Advertiser*, p. 5.

[283] "$1 Million in Land Sales Every Month on or around Hindmarsh Island." *The Advertiser*, May 14, 2001: p. 9.

The fact or fiction of the "women's business" was a major point of contention. Robert Tonkinson states in the beginning of "Anthropology and Aboriginal Tradition" that the Hindmarsh Island Bridge Affair may be the first and definitely the most widely publicized case in which "allegations of Aboriginal cultural knowledge have been made . . . publicly by Aboriginal people."[284] The Ngarrindjeri number around 3000, although they are somewhat scattered. The largest concentration resides in Roukkan (formerly known as Point McLeay) located in the Lower Murray area. Tonkinson goes on to write, "given the high degree of diversity of Ngarrindjeri experiences, these would inevitably be varying local understandings concerning "tradition."[285]

This issue of diversity is important because it begs the question of whose statements concerning the "women's business" should be believed—the proponent women's or the dissident women's? Weiner writes in "Culture in a Sealed Envelope" that a major part of the Royal Commission's conclusion of fabrication were anthropological assessments from as far back as the 1940s. These reports made no mention of the "women's business", and stated that the lack of female sacred sites was the way in which the Ngarrindjeri differed from other Aboriginal societies in Australia.[286] However, Betty Fisher, an Aboriginal woman, did give evidence to the commission that she had recorded statements of Ngarrindjeri elder women during the 1960s and that they mentioned the "women's business" to her at that time.[287] She was not an anthropologist, and this leads to another point of contention regarding the Commission: the knowledge of experts versus the knowledge of the group.

Deane Fergie, the anthropologist who was originally hired by the ALRM and was the first to report the claims of "women's business," pointed out that there were "more non-Aboriginal people who appeared as witnesses than Aboriginal people" and that the proponent women boycotted the Commission with one exception. She defended her findings and attacked the Commission's findings in "Secret Envelopes and Inferential

---

[284] Robert Tonkinson (1997). "Anthropology and Aboriginal Tradition: The Hindmarsh Island Bridge Affair and the Politics of Interpretation." *Oceania*, 68(1): 1.

[285] Ibid., p. 9.

[286] James F. Weiner (1999). "Culture in a Sealed Envelope: The Concealment of Australian Aboriginal Heritage and Tradition in the Hindmarsh Island Bridge Affair." *The Journal of the Royal Anthropological Institute*, 5(2): 198.

[287] Mary Elizabeth Fisher (1996). "Subservience, Concealment and Impudence." *Journal of Australian Studies*, 48: 52. Diane Bell's 1998 book, *Ngarrindjeri Wurruwarrin: A World that Is, Was and Will Be* (Melbourne: Spinifex Press, 1998), supports the claims of the proponent women.

Tautologies." James Weiner, in a 1997 article, criticized Fergie's findings because she placed too much importance on the remarks of the spokesperson for the proponent women when making her assessments. She reported to the Commission that she did not need to test the claims because she believed her source.[288]

Dr. Fergie's sources, the proponent women of the Ngarrindjeri, were scrutinized as well. Doreen Kartinyeri claimed to have received the knowledge from an older Ngarrindjeri woman and "most of [the proponent women] had no knowledge of the existence of Ngarrindjeri women's business prior to 1993 when they met with Doreen Kartinyeri to hear her version of it."[289] Anthropologist Marcia Langton defended the proponent women, and stated that Aboriginal women who adhere to the local Aboriginal beliefs have sacred sites and rituals that are associated only with women.[290]

Although it is recognized that many Aboriginal groups have sites sacred only to women, many experts (such as two museum curators, Clarke and Jones) testified to the Commission that it is an impossibility for "women's business" to have existed among the Ngarrindjeri before the bridge affair.[291] Langton, however, quotes a statement made on behalf of the proponent women before the Royal Commission in which the authority of the Royal Commission is denied and asserted that "we [the proponent women] know women's business exists and is true."[292]

The focus on the validity of the claims and the deference given to anthropologists over the proponent women in this case seemed fueled by skepticism from the larger society. The bridge and the development were to be a boon to the local economy. The state government had already committed itself to a large monetary sum before the women's claims were investigated. The sites found before and during construction were not enough to warrant stopping the project. Evidently the proponent women were at a disadvantage from the start. The lack of unity from the women of the Ngarrindijeri combined with the secret nature of the "women's business" contributed to suspicion regarding the women's claims from the beginning of the Hindmarsh Affair. The public and the media seemed predisposed to disbelief.

---

[288] James F. Weiner (1997). "Must Our Informants Mean What They Say?" *Canberra Anthropology*, 20(1 and 2): 83.

[289] Ibid., p. 89.

[290] Supra n275, p. 212.

[291] Steve Hemming (1996). "Inventing Ethnography." *Journal of Australian Studies*, p. 25.

[292] Supra n275, p. 214.

Sacred Sites Litigation in Australia

The legal claim by the proponent women that the bridge would cause a spiritual injury is better understood when Australia's treatment of sacred sites is examined. Australia, unlike similar states, has developed a body of specialized law relating to cultural heritage. Federal and state legislation passed in the 1970s and 1980s recognized Aboriginal sacred sites not only in terms of objects and human-constructed cultural heritage, but also natural sites. These laws "acknowledg[ed] the continuing importance of traditional sites to Aboriginal people."[293] The first type of legislation to develop for the protection of Aboriginal sacred sites was mainly concerned with "cultural relics."[294] The protection of "relics" in early legislation emphasized Aboriginal culture as a thing of the past, as opposed to being ongoing and continually changing.[295]

Although the Hindmarsh Affair took place in South Australia, there have been several similar Aboriginal land claims in the Northern Territory,[296] as well as several pieces of legislation.[297] The best example is the Coronation Hill dispute.[298] The Aboriginal applicants in the Coronation Hill case were similar to the proponent women in the Hindmarsh Affair because they both claimed a sacred site that would be injured, but not in a physical sense. In this case, the injury would occur due to the mining. Also, other members of the Jawoyn community supported the mining venture.[299] This 1991 case, as Ian Keen pointed out, illustrated the intersection of the competing interests of commercial development, environmental concerns, and the rights of indigenous people.[300] The Jawoyn believed the

---

[293] David Ritchie (1994). "Principles and Practice of Site Protection Laws in Australia." In David L. Carmichael, Jane Hubert, Brian Reeves, and Audhild Schanche (Eds.) (1994). *Sacred Sites, Sacred Places*. London; New York: Routledge, p. 227.

[294] Ibid.

[295] Ibid., p. 228.

[296] Supra n275, p. 215.

[297] Supra n293, p. 239.

[298] Another important case relating to Aboriginal rights is *Mabo v The State of Queensland*. In this landmark 1992 High Court decision, the presumption of *terra nullius* regarding how the state acquired land was overturned. Indigenous people in Australia were acknowledged as the previous owners who did not give up their customary rights to the land. Barbara Hocking (1993). "Aboriginal Law Does Now Run in Australia." *Sydney Law Review*, 15: 187-205. For a more complete account of this judgment, see *Sydney Law Review*, 15(2) 1993. This issue is dedicated to the *Mabo* decision.

[299] Supra n275, p. 216.

[300] Ian Keen (1993). "Aboriginal Beliefs vs. Mining at Coronation Hill: The Containing Force of Traditionalism." *Human Organization*, 52(4): 344.

land would be hurt in a non-physical sense. Even if the actual geographical locale was untouched, mining—and, more specifically, blasting—might disturb Bula, their creator. "[T]he results [would] be catastrophic, there [would] become sick and [would] die."[301]

In the Hindmarsh Island Bridge Affair, the claims were suspect because there was no agreement about the existence of the secret "women's business." However, the Jawoyn people were not unified in their position on the mining venture either. Young Jawoyns and older Jawoyns disagreed, especially since some of the younger Jawoyns worked for the mining company.[302] There were also dissenters among the Jawoyns who did not believe the mining would harm Bula.[303] The issue of diversity of opinion within a group presented a problem to the court, which then sought to identify the "true" story. Because of the need for a definitive account of the Jawoyns beliefs, anthropologists debated the validity of the Jawoyns' claim. In question was how long they had held these beliefs and why no objection was made to a previous mining operation in the 1960s.[304] "The voices of Jawoyn were seldom heard during the debate. The process treated them largely as objects of discourse rather than agents."[305]

Although the Coronation Hill dispute was similar to the Hindmarsh Island Bridge Affair in that they both involved a sacred site threatened with non-physical harm and at the heart of both cases was the question of validity, they differed in a key way—Coronation Hill did not involve claims of "women's business." There have been other land claims concerning the sacred sites of women in Australia, but none have received as much attention as Ngarrindjeri claims regarding Hindmarsh Island. In the early 1980s, Arrente women created a great deal of publicity by opposing the construction of a dam. Some disclosure of the site's significance was required by the government in order to validate their claim.[306] It was their decision to publicize the information concerning the "Two Women Dreaming" site. The publicity created worldwide support for the women, but

---

[301] Ibid., p. 346.

[302] Jane M. Jacobs (1993). "'Shake 'im this Country': The mapping of the Aboriginal Sacred in Australia—The Case of Coronation Hill." In Peter Jackson and Jan Penrose (Eds.) (1993). *Constructions of Race, Place and Nation*, London: UCL Press, 103.

[303] Supra n300, p. 352.

[304] Ibid. See also the similar Hindmarsh claim concerning the introduction of a ferry.

[305] Ibid., p. 345.

[306] Ken Gelder and Jane M. Jacobs (1995). "'Talking Out of Place': Authorizing the Aboriginal Sacred in Postcolonial Australia." *Cultural Studies*, 9(1): 154.

some Arrente women were displeased with the public accessibility to information that had once been restricted.[307]

There have been several instances of female land claims, but the process has been mostly male dominated. Female land claims and claims of "women's business" have become more common since female anthropologists and female field workers began working for the Land Council in the Northern Territory. "Women's business" is considered a topic traditionally only to be discussed with other women, and their reluctance to share this information with men or reveal it in the presence of women is due to its revelation going against the customary practice of secrecy regarding this information.[308]

The controversy in the Hindmarsh Affair centered around the validity of the proponent women's claims. It can be argued that the claims were considered highly suspect because they were made by women and did not come from the both men and women of the Aboriginal society as in the Coronation Hill Dispute.[309] A key aspect of the Hindmarsh case, as has been stated earlier in this paper, was the high level of disagreement among the Ngarrindjeri women. Perhaps assuming all the Ngarrindjeri women should be unified is also unfair. There was dissension in the Coronation Hill Dispute, but that did not prevent the Court from ruling in favor of the Jawoyns opposed to the mining.

Individual Rights vs. Group Rights

The majority of the human rights codified in international law are those that pertain to individuals only. This idea of rights as something that the individual possesses is also enshrined in the legal domestic legal systems of most Western nation-states. While the emphasis in human rights documents has been placed on individual rights, there are provisions that protect group rights as well. Group rights are inherently those rights that can only be exercised and enjoyed by a collective. Examples of such rights are the right to culture and the right to self-determination. Because legal systems including the Human Rights Committee in the United

---

[307] Ibid., p. 155.

[308] Meredith Rowell (1983). "Women and Land Claims in the Northern Territory." In Nicholas Peterson and Marcia Langton (Eds.) (1983). *Aborigines, Land and Land Rights.* Canberra: Australian Institute of Aboriginal Studies, p. 262.

[309] Joanna Bourke (1997). "Women's Business: Sex, Secrets and the Hindmarsh Island Affair." *UNSW Law Journal,* 20(2): 340. Bourke's article suggests that the interplay of sexism and racism had a role in the outcome of this dispute. The article makes important distinctions between the perceived credibility of men in recent sacred sites cases and that of the women in the Hindmarsh Affair.

Nations are set up to protect and recognize mainly individual rights, the legal systems cannot "fully address the concerns of those intent on preserving the integrity of their groups."[310] Adjudicating group claims on the international level is difficult because "states themselves are the dominant players within the international law system."[311] The state requires a group to prove its claims, which can be at times antithetical to that group's own customary laws and traditional beliefs, as in the Hindmarsh Affair and the Coronation Hill dispute. Indigenous people are a challenge to these systems. Identifying the group and the proper representative of the group can be difficult.[312] The focus on individual rights in the international human rights instruments is posited upon the assumption that the protection of groups is accomplished through the protection of the rights of the individual members.[313] What this premise fails to account for is that the rights which groups retain cannot be protected through allowing their protection on an individual level. The right to culture is a right for the enjoyment of a group.

Cultural Rights and Gender

While the Hindmarsh Affair did involve this conflict of claims of group rights in a legal system created to adjudicate claims of individual rights, it is not purely a group rights claim. Gender was also a major component. Did the Ngarrindjeri women have a right to protect their cultural heritage? According to past claims in Australia and the laws, Aboriginal women in Australia do have the right to their own cultural heritage, which is separate from that of Aboriginal men in some instances. The Court never decided the question of the validity of the women's claims or their cultural rights. In fact, Chief Justice Doyle stated that in making his decision regarding the Royal Commission that he "assume[d], without deciding, that the inquiry w[ould] in fact intrude upon the freedom of certain Ngarrindjeri people to hold and practice their religion," due to the fact that it would force them to

---

[310] Richard Herz (1993). "Legal Protection for Indigenous Cultures: Sacred Sites and Communal Rights. *Virginia Law Review*, 79(3): 697.

[311] Ibid., p. 694.

[312] Gordon Bennett (1978). *Aboriginal rights in International Law*. London: Anthropological Institute [for] Survival International, p. 51.

[313] Ian Brownlie (1992). *Treaties and Indigenous Peoples*. Oxford: Clarendon Press; New York: Oxford University Press, 36. See also Chandran Kukathas (1992), "Are There any Cultural Rights?" *Political Theory*, 20(1): 105-139; and Will Kymlicka (1995), *Multicultural Citizenship: A Liberal Theory of Minority Rights*. Oxford: Clarendon Press. As noted supra n53, Kukathas argues that right to association should be the framework in which cultural rights are discussed and that the right to culture is not a separate right. Kukathas argues against group rights, whereas Kymlicka supports them.

have their beliefs examined and their secrets disclosed.[314] The judge did not feel that this was enough to prohibit the inquiry, and validating the claims was considered more important.

The proponent women in the Hindmarsh Affair were claiming a specific right to both their heritage and their religion which would be only applicable to Ngarrindjeri women. Although there was disagreement among Ngarrindjeri women, the harm of the spiritual injury could only be to Ngarrindjeri women. The lack of state protection for a harm inflicted by the state (allowing the building of the bridge) created a situation in which the proponent women could not invoke clear existing human rights law. The human rights enshrined in the international instruments grant rights to both women and men, but a redefinition of traditional human rights concepts is required for women to access their rights.[315] For women to be able to fully access their right to religion, states have to recognize the women's fundamental right to do so.

Concerns over individual rights do not necessarily outweigh the rights of the group.[316] An example of this point is the case of *Sandra Lovelace v. Canada* mentioned in Chapter 1. Sandra Lovelace was a member of the Maliseet Indian tribe in Canada. She married a non-member in 1970 and subsequently lost her status as an Indian under Canada's Indian Act. This provision only applied to women who married non-Indians. She submitted a communication to the Human Rights Committee in 1977 stating that this was a violation of the *International Covenant of Civil and Political Rights*. The HRC would not rule on the matter of her lost nationality, because her marriage took place before Canada was bound by the ICCPR, but it did recognize that the loss of her nationality still affected the enjoyment of her human rights on the basis of sex.

---

[314] *The Aboriginal Legal Rights Movement, Inc. v. The State of South Australia and Iris Eliza Stevens* (1995). 64 ASR 551.

[315] For an extended discussion of women's human rights, see J. Oloka-Onyango and Sylvia Tamale (1995), "'The Personal is Political,' or Why Women's Rights are Indeed Human Rights: An African Perspective on International Feminism," *Human Rights Quarterly*, 17(4): 691-731; Laura Reanda (1981), "Human Rights and Women's Rights: The United Nations Approach," *Human Rights Quarterly*, 3(2): 11-31; Hilary Charlesworth (1994), "What Are 'Women's International Human Rights'?," in Rebecca J. Cook (Ed.), *Human Rights of Women: National and International Perspectives* (pp. 532-571); and Charlotte Bunch (1990), "Women's Rights as Human Rights: Toward a Re-Vision of Human Rights," *Human Rights Quarterly*, 12(4): 486-498.

[316] Bahia Tahzib-Lie (1999). "Applying a Gender Perspective in the Area of the Right to Freedom of Religion or Belief." *Brigham Young University Law Review*, 1999: 967. This article addresses the ways in which women's rights to enjoy and participate in their religion and freedom of belief are limited by states under the auspices of their protection.

During the adjudication of this matter, Lovelace's marriage ended and she wanted the right to rejoin her tribe, which the HRC granted on the basis of Article 27 of the ICCPR.[317] This decision was extremely significant because it involved the debate between the rights of the individual and the rights of the group, and also the debate between gender and culture. By not deciding the matter regarding the original loss of nationality, the HRC was spared from having to choose between two human rights, much like the Australian Courts never have had to rule on the validity of the proponent women's beliefs in the Hindmarsh Affair. What the HRC did state through its decision is that people have a right to enjoy their culture. The original decision under Canadian law which caused Lovelace to lose her nationality recognized the tribe's right to their customary law as more important than the individual rights of Lovelace. Lovelace's individual rights had to be balanced with those of the community.

At the center of the Hindmarsh Affair is also an issue of customary law. A major point of contention over the claims of "women's business" has been that Ngarrindjeri women disagree over its existence, which begs the question: who is the proper representative of the group? This plagues both national and international legal systems. The Human Rights Committee, for example, has no submission process for communications on behalf of groups, only states and individuals. The Australian government sought to answer this question through the Royal Commission, but the proper remedy would be to adhere to the customary law of the Ngarrindjeri and to let the indigenous group decide upon its proper representatives.

Human Rights in International Law

Australian law regarding cultural heritage is very developed and specific. State legislation (such as the *Aboriginal Heritage Act* from South Australia and the *Northern Territory Land Rights Act*) "conferred rights with respect to sites on the traditional Aboriginal custodians of these sites."[318] *The Aboriginal and Torres Strait Islander Heritage Protection Act* (known as *The Heritage Protection Act*) is probably the most important piece of Australian legislation in this area. It allows the protection of "a significant Aboriginal area" that is also threatened with harm and it

---

[317] *Sandra Lovelace v. Canada.* Communication No. R.6/24. Views of the Human Rights Committee. Report of the Human Rights Committee, Annex XVIII. General Assembly Official Records, 36th Session, Supplement No. 40 (A/36/40). New York: United Nations, 1981.

[318] Supra n293, p. 237.

allows for claims to be brought by or on behalf of a group of indigenous people.[319]

Both Australian law and the UNESCO *Convention for the Protection of the World Cultural and Natural Heritage,* recognize cultural heritage as human-constructed objects and places as well as natural areas that have significance to a particular group.[320] However, Article 4 states that countries should identify and protect areas of cultural heritage "to the utmost of its own resources."[321] This stands in contrast to the Australian law, which ultimately was judged to be insufficient to stop the South Australian parliament from passing the Hindmarsh Island Bridge Act in 1997. This Act forbade any further application under the Heritage Protection Act that would seek to stop the bridge construction.

While the claims of "women's business" are disputed in the Hindmarsh Affair, it is clear that the island holds significance for the Ngarrindjeri people and that "women's business" exists, at least to the proponent women. The *UN Declaration on the Rights of Indigenous Peoples* states in Article 12 that "indigenous peoples have the right to manifest, practise, develop and teach their spiritual and religious traditions, customs and ceremonies[,]" as well as "have access in privacy to their religious and cultural sites" which states have an obligation to protect.[322] Article 13 of this same document states that indigenous people have the right to "revitalize their cultural traditions and customs" which includes the right to develop and maintain sacred sites.[323] This document is a declaration adopted by the UN General Assembly; however, it explains the rights of indigenous people in great detail and illustrates how the Ngarrindjeri have not been given the right to develop or assert any cultural heritage. The Australian government required proof that this was an old belief, but nothing in international human rights law states that indigenous people are disallowed from developing and changing their cultural traditions and beliefs.

Although the Declaration is not legally binding, as is the case with declarations generally, the *International Covenant on Economic, Social, and*

---

[319] Supra n266, sections 9 and 10.

[320] United Nations Educational, Scientific, and Cultural Organization. (1972). *Convention for the Protection of the World Cultural and Natural Heritage.* Paris: United Nations. Entered into force on Dec. 17, 1975. Articles 1 and 2.

[321] Ibid., Article 4.

[322] *United Nations Declaration on the Rights of Indigenous Peoples.* UN Doc. A/RES/61/295, Article 12.

[323] Ibid., Article 13. Other important articles in this document are Articles 19 and 25.

Cultural Rights (the ICESCR) and the ICCPR are legally enforceable. Article 1(1) of the ICESCR states that "all people have the right to self-determination. By virtue of that right they freely determine their political status and freely pursue their economic, social and cultural development."[324] Article 27 of the ICCPR states that members of an ethnic minority "shall not be denied the right, in community with other members of their group, to enjoy their own culture [and] to profess and practice their own religion."[325] However, as Jeremy Waldron points out, Article 27 grants these collective rights without a clear definition of the terms.[326] Groups cannot access their human rights because the laws have been created with a bias towards individuals. If the members of the Ngarrindjeri society who opposed the building of the bridge had sought to bring their claims of human rights violations to the United Nations, they would have encountered the same problems as they faced in Australia. There was no mechanism for group claims in existence. Any mechanism created for the purpose of settling the conflict would have to deal with the difficult issue of deciding who spoke for the group. In this case members of the indigenous people have argued over this point, and the dissension among them further fueled the belief that the claims carried no validity.

Most significantly, the Hindmarsh Affair is an example of a claim of a collective right to women's culture. Although not fully articulated in these terms, it is an example of a gendered cultural rights claim, for which there is also no redressability under *The Convention on the Elimination of All Forms of Discrimination Against Women* (the *Women's Convention*). There is no mechanism for group complaints in the *Optional Protocol*, and the *Women's Convention* does not address cultural rights. It contains provisions for allowing women to access their equal rights with men. The convention is written in individual terms and neither the issue of minority culture nor women's cultural participation in minority culture is addressed. In the final analysis, no legal instrument afforded protection of their rights.

---

[324] United Nations (1966). *International Covenant on Economic, Social and Cultural Rights.* In Ian Brownlie (Ed.) (1995). *Basic Documents in International Law, 4th ed.* Oxford: Clarendon Press, Art. 1(1), p. 264.

[325] United Nations (1966). International Covenant on Civil and Political Rights. In Ian Brownlie (Ed.) (1995). *Basic Documents in International Law, 4th ed.* Oxford: Clarendon Press, pp. 276-297, Article 27.

[326] Jeremy Waldron (1995). "Minority Cultures and the Cosmopolitan Alternative." In Will Kymlicka (Ed.) (1995). *The Rights of Minority Cultures.* New York: Oxford University Press, p. 97.

Implications of the Hindmarsh Island Bridge Affair

The Hindmarsh Island Bridge Affair generated a great deal of controversy for decades. The proponent women and other Ngarrindjeri were determined to fight the bridge construction as the government of South Australia was to build it. The validity of the claims of secret "women's business" remains a matter of debate in the area. While Ngarrindjeri women disagree about its existence, the proponent women's assertions should not be discounted, especially given the treatment of similar cases like Coronation Hill. International human rights law does not state that a cultural belief must be held by every member of the group. It should not be for the court or the government of Australia or any other state to decide who are the rightful representatives of the group; that matter should be decided within the culture according to their own customary law. Also, the amount of time that a group has held a belief or site sacred should not be of utmost importance. This denies the society or culture the right to change and develop, which are made explicit in the *Draft Declaration on the Rights of Indigenous Peoples*. Whatever the amount of time that Hindmarsh Island has been sacred, it is definitely of significance to the Ngarrindjeri now.

The Hindmarsh Island Bridge Affair also attests to the fact that government is not always an impartial arbiter. The South Australia government had a vested interest in the construction of the bridge. It had pledged funds for its building, and the accompanying marina was expected to prop up the sagging local economy, which it has in recent months. When the federal government appeared to be more favorable to the Ngarrindjeri people (through Minister Tickner's original ban and the short-lived appointment of Justice Jane Matthews to write a new report), the state parliament stepped in and passed a law prohibiting any further litigation under the Heritage Protection Act. They let their bias be known. Also, the legal system is set up in such a way that the human rights of the Ngarrindjeri cannot be fully protected. Now that former Minister Tickner has been ordered to read the sealed report, it is clear that the courts do not respect the customs and wishes of the people whose culture they discuss.

Western law, including international law, has been created to deal with claims of individual rights. But these rights have used male-centered as the definition of universal and equal. The Hindmarsh Affair challenges both premises, but, surprisingly, neither the issues in this case nor the human rights concerns can be addressed fully by the *Women's Convention*. Although the case involves a gendered claim on a sacred site, the heart of the case is an issue of indigenous rights and the right to develop, change, and maintain culture. It is a hybrid of competing claims of women's and cultural rights, and the case cannot be fully examined nor rights fully protected without looking directly at gendered cultural rights.

While the latter is often characterized as limiting the rights of women (as seen in the *Lovelace* case), the Hindmarsh Island Bridge Affair shows that women also want the right to maintain and participate in their own cultures, and that there can be disagreement within a group on how this can be achieved. The issues of validity and authenticity that minority groups such as the Ngarrindjeri have had to contend with are major facets of this case because they exist as a minority culture.

This case indicates that even when the legal systems of Western, multicultural states attempt to acknowledge group rights and diversity among its citizens, they fail to understand that diversity of opinion and culture can exist within that group that, by its very existence, creates pluralism within the nation's population. Some scholars would argue that this problem could easily be remedied by only acknowledging individual rights. However, culture, already recognized as a human right, cannot exist only in individual forms. Culture belongs to the group and is a defining characteristic of a community.

Australia's specialized body of law relating to indigenous peoples does more to protect group rights than similarly situated countries, but, as this case proves, it does not do enough—nor do United Nations human rights treaties. The claim of a gendered cultural rights or sacred site has not been addressed in law, and neither have other issues of group rights claims such as standing and proving authenticity. The Hindmarsh Island Bridge Affair illustrates that women's rights and cultural rights need not be in competition with one another. This case, unlike the others examined, shows the women seeking to invoke a collective right. The category of gendered cultural rights does not currently exist in either national or international law. No existing legal categories were sufficient for their claims. Although there was skepticism from the larger society over the gendered nature of the claim and the existence of dissent within the Ngarrindjeri, the existence of a rights category specifically for claims such as women's right to culture may have affected the outcome of this case.

Recognizing the relationship between gender and cultural rights can give rise to a category of human rights which would specifically examine women's cultural rights, and which could offer greater protection to women as they make rights claims. The Hindmarsh Island Affair illustrates that not only is conceptual recognition important, but women must also have adequate mechanisms available through which to invoke their rights. If this recognition of gendered cultural rights is not given, women may not be able to fit their claims into other rights categories. The existence of a mechanism alone is insufficient to guarantee consideration of women's cultural rights if there does not already exist a category of gendered cultural rights into which women can fit their claims. The realization that, because of the challenges women face in accessing their human rights, particular mechanisms are necessary to ensure their protection is a rationale for the *Convention on the Elimination of All Forms of Discrimination against Women*. The same is true for the interconnection between gender and culture. If in the Hindmarsh example, women's cultural rights claims must fit into the established mechanisms for addressing cultural rights claims, this may not be adequate for women's cultural claims.

6

RECOGNIZING A WOMAN'S RIGHT TO CULTURE: IMPLICATIONS AND CONCLUSIONS

Neither cultural, religious, nor gender rights are fully protected in multicultural Western states where governments discuss rights and rights protection the most. Looking at the connection between gender and culture for claims from minority women shows the need not only to acknowledge this interconnectivity, but actually to see a category born of the inherent intersection. This rights category shows the need to have a more nuanced understanding of gendered cultural rights in order to create better solutions to conflicts between the minority and majority culture over issues of gender. The headscarf debate in France demonstrates the need for a category of gendered cultural rights and a focus on women's right to religion as an agent of culture. The issue of the *get* in New York shows the difficulties of crafting a solution and the problems with the exit option. The *Holyfield* case further complicates the exit option. It appears to be the most likely case for supporting women's individual rights against culture, yet upon closer inspection challenges the assumptions of the relationship between gender and culture. The Hindmarsh Island Bridge Affair shows the utility of the category of women's cultural rights, as well as the problems with ascertaining the accuracy of claims with invocation of this right in the absence of international human rights law.

Although the examples have come from women in minority religions and cultures, it is not my intention to further Western stereotypes by examining religion and culture as purely aspects of minority life. Religion and culture exist for the majority, too. However, the dominant in society have the privilege or disadvantage of seeing their own way of life as natural or normal, with everyone else judged accordingly. Scholars and human rights activists could examine this chart and interpret it as supporting claims that cultural rights are inherently detrimental to women. However, I contend that it is useful to show why a gendered approach to cultural rights allows for an understanding of how women in minority cultures are left out of the protection of women's human rights or the right to culture. Women's rights are at risk when they must be negotiated through both the larger society and the minority culture because they do not have a mechanism or language in which to discuss the protection of their rights as female members of a cultural community. For the state to fully protect women's human rights and cultural rights, it must: 1) recognize the gendered nature of cultural rights—that the ways in which men and women participate in their cultural and religious communities differ, and 2) integrate this understanding into the drafting of legislation and judicial decisions so that the state does not discriminate against women by ignoring their cultural rights. If we do not recognize a woman's right to culture, human rights will have failed both women and minorities.

Policy Implementation

The integration of gendered cultural rights into international human rights law and policy is crucial to success. While the use of gendered cultural rights ultimately is key to addressing perceived rights controversies within national contexts, an international understanding of this rights category would designate gendered cultural rights legitimacy as a human right. It would allow women to connect gendered cultural rights claims to broader human rights issues. Not only would this create an international legal space for human rights claims, it would open human rights advocacy to gendered cultural rights issues. Activism on behalf of gendered cultural rights could build human rights awareness on issues previously perceived to be outside of human rights claims. It could also spur local legal systems to address gendered cultural rights.

Because human rights organizations such as Amnesty International and Human Rights Watch follow the lead of the United Nations in international human rights, women making gendered cultural rights claims will find few allies in the human rights community before international recognition. For policy integration to begin at the international level, the participation of United Nations treaty bodies is necessary. The treaty bodies interpret the international human rights conventions, setting the international tone for the human rights contained in each treaty. For example, the Committee on the Elimination of All Forms of Discrimination against Women (CEDAW), the treaty body of the Women's Convention, addressed violence against women in General Recommendation 19 as violation of women's human rights, enumerating several specific human rights denied through gender-based violence.[327] Clearly defining violence against women as a human rights concern has allowed for human rights activism on this

---

[327] Committee on the Elimination of All Forms of Discrimination against Women. General Recommendation 19. UN Doc. A/47/38.

issue, pressuring state action on specific concerns in this area.[328] Gendered cultural rights would benefit from treaty bodies crafting recommendations on this subject. Scholars have argued for treaty bodies other than CEDAW to fully examine the issue of gender with an eye to integrating gender into the treaties through recommendations.[329] But while it is important for treaty bodies to examine gender as well as culture, the issue of gendered cultural rights will not be fully integrated without the issuance of recommendations examining the gendered dimensions of cultural rights.

Although a general recommendation should come from CEDAW, a recommendation on this issue should not be confined to one committee. Ideally, gendered cultural rights should be integrated into each of the human rights conventions that address culture as well as gender. Two ways in which gendered cultural rights could be addressed in relation to the right to culture are: 1) a comment from the Human Rights Committee of the *International Covenant on Civil and Political Rights* on Article 27, and 2) a comment from the Committee on Economic, Social and Cultural Rights on Article 15 of the *International Covenant on Economic, Social and Cultural Rights*. Furthermore, because of the many reservations by states to *The Convention on All Forms of Discrimination against Women*, it may be more difficult to pressure states to protect gendered cultural rights. This is particularly true if the interpretation of this human right is confined to the human rights convention with so many reservations. An additional problem is that some states have not ratified it, including the United States. Once it is adopted at the international level, state parties can be asked to report their compliance with the protection of gendered cultural rights in their reporting to treaty bodies such as the Human Rights Committee.

The category of gendered cultural rights, once it is adopted at the international level, could open issues such as those discussed in the previous chapters to a human rights approach, and also could provide a critical

---

[328] There has been substantial action on this rights issue. Transnational and local non-governmental organizations have addressed it. For example, the Amnesty International Stop Violence Against Women Campaign is a worldwide human rights campaign calling on governments to enact and/or enforce laws to protect women from specific forms of violence. See www.amnesty.org.

[329] Dianne Otto has argued for a comment from the Committee on Economic, Social and Cultural Rights, and also the examination of previous comments from the United Nations treaty bodies. See Dianne Otto (2002). "'Gender Comment': Why Does the UN Committee on Economic, Social, and Cultural Rights Need a General Comment on Women?" *Canadian Journal of Women and the Law*, 14: 1-52.

connection between international human rights law and national action.[330] At a national level, states should endeavor to protect gendered cultural rights. Similar to the Australian attempt to protect cultural rights explored in the discussion of the Hindmarsh Island Bridge Affair, states should provide institutional mechanisms through which women can bring claims of gendered cultural rights. However, as the Hindmarsh case illustrates, the existence of a mechanism alone may not be adequate if gendered cultural rights are not fully recognized. A combination of actions may be necessary to create a comprehensive national approach to address gendered cultural rights. The example of the *get* in New York shows the need for a multifaceted approach. Because this is an issue of divorce, an area normally regulated by states instead of the federal government, it has been left to the state legislature and state judiciary to craft solutions. Additionally, the issue of the *get* highlights the importance of activism within the community and in the broader society.

Employing a human rights approach through the lens of gendered cultural rights would not guarantee a particular outcome in a rights controversy. However, without the ability for women to invoke gendered cultural rights in legal arenas or through activism, the perception of inherent tension between women's human rights and the right to culture will continue to produce scenarios in which women are forced to make an unfair choice between their identities as women and members of a culture. A gendered cultural rights approach opens new possibilities for women that cannot exist under the current rights categorization in which gender and culture are diametrically opposed.

Research Implications

An argument for gendered cultural rights shows the complexity of the relationship between women's rights and the right to culture, and also addresses a subject that has been ignored in the group rights and gender literature. The implications of this argument are crucial for both human rights jurisprudence and policy. While scholarly debates continue about the nature of human rights and about the relative priority of rights, this studyshows that rights can be mutually reinforcing. Understanding the

---

[330] Elsa Stamatopoulou examines how cultural rights have been protected under international law and provides recommendations for the further protection of cultural rights in international and national frameworks. The focus of the work is cultural rights even though Stamatopoulou recognizes that gender and culture are not always at odds. With an understanding of gendered cultural rights, these recommendations can be adapted to fully integrate gendered cultural rights into national and international contexts. See Elsa Stamatopoulou (2007). *Cultural Rights in International Law: Article 27 of the Universal Declaration of Human Rights and Beyond*. Leiden: Martinus Nifjhoff Publishers.

delicate and intricate relationship between gender and culture shows a need for recognition of gendered cultural rights in international law. Neither the Women's Convention nor the ICCPR or the ICESCR acknowledge or seek to remedy the dearth of provisions protecting gendered culture. These conventions reflect the human rights jurisprudence influenced by individualistic conceptions of human rights and an assumption that culture is detrimental to women.

In addition to enriching international law, a revised understanding of gender and culture could create new space in which to advocate and defend human rights. There is often a disconnect between international human rights activists, as well as and Western feminists, and local women. Focusing on issues of gendered culture could allow for a discovery of common ground. Because gendered cultural rights are an additional avenue for advancing human rights claims, there is space for both claims that seek to retain aspects of a society that women find empowering and for claims for greater equality and participation within the community. This approach could help to transform local concerns into the language of international human rights and bridge a long-standing gap between these groups, and a gendered approach to cultural rights is a response to critics of women's movements as detrimental to culture.[331] This allows women to work collectively within their communities for change, but acknowledges the importance of local culture.

This investigation of women's cultural rights claims, in response to work in Western feminist theory, illustrates the more complex relationship between gender and culture, a relationship which has been oversimplified. The binary opposition presumed to exist between gender and culture has been challenged somewhat by scholars concerned with multiculturalism and gender such as Ayelet Shachar and Sarah Song, but the core tension between gender and cultural rights remains. Much of this literature is focused on proposing solutions to these challenges of balancing competing rights in a plural society, but they do not employ a human rights approach. I do not deny that there are examples of the interaction between gender rights and culture in which these human rights are at odds. However, I

---

[331] For further discussion of the relationship between local human rights groups and transnational organizations, see Margaret E. Keck and Kathryn Sikkink (1998). *Activists Beyond Borders: Advocacy Networks in International Politics.* Ithaca, NY: Cornell University Press. Annelise Riles takes a different perspective on the nature of the advocacy network in her study of women's development groups in the Pacific. Annelise Riles (2000). *The Network Inside Out.* Ann Arbor: University of Michigan Press. See also Sally Merry (2006). *Human Rights and Gender Violence.* Chicago: University of Chicago Press.

argue that because this work appears to presume a tension between these rights, a category of rights is obscured: women's cultural rights.

The political theory and multiculturalism literature could also benefit from a more complex analysis of gender and culture. Too often the focus of this work is the relationship between the majority and minority culture without fully investigating the issue of gender. For both of these overlapping literatures, this book can offer an example of the use of empirical evidence in the form of the extended case method to elucidate theoretical claims. Theoretical works incorporating empirical evidence like those of Siobhan Mullally, Sarah Song, and Ayelet Shachar are encouraging. However, more in-depth analysis of the cases through a lens of gendered cultural rights can produce a richer picture of the controversy and the implications for women's cultural rights.

The study of women's human rights has often followed a parallel course to that of feminist theory. I incorporate feminist theory and multiculturalism into a human rights project in order to show that these literatures are beneficial to one another. This work shows the importance of combining theoretical work with international law in order to find human rights concerns that have been missed by the current categorization of women's rights and cultural rights.

Like women's identity, cultural rights are important to the study of religion. Taking women's cultural rights into account opens a new avenue by which to explore religious freedom. The headscarf affair in France, the issue of the *get*, and the Hindmarsh affair all illustrate aspects of this relationship. Yet, a key thread connecting these chapters is the right of women to fully become part of their religions—and how this effort can best be supported in the larger society.

Most importantly, this work has implications for law and society work and for political science. In the area of law and society, this study illustrates the benefits of using a human rights framework to explore cross-national legal questions. The analysis of the cases allows for an examination of legal decisions and for the understanding of and use of the law by women, as well as analysis of the impact of policy decisions. The *Holyfield* case, for example, shows the importance of examining the impact of these decisions—the woman did not win in the United States Supreme Court. However, she did eventually get her preferred outcome—her children were adopted outside of the tribe. For political science, this work shows the importance of interdisciplinary research for examining identity and political conflicts within multicultural, Western states.

Culture is not limited to minority groups. Women from all backgrounds should take to heart the idea of gendered cultural rights, because it can give all women a new avenue for human rights claims. This idea can support women's human rights and the right to one's culture. It can serve to highlight complex relationships and bring to light further human rights questions. Women should look around them for the empowering aspects of their societies. In the United States, this could be a new way to argue for women's sports or single-sex education, as well as traditionally female activities like quilting bees.

Approaching cultural rights through gender does not have to apply only to women. Men, too, have cultural rights, and there may be activities within a society that could fit this category. I have limited my discussion of gender and cultural rights to women because, in patriarchal societies, men's rights are already far more likely to receive greater protection. Gendered culture should not be a defense against discriminatory policies nor should human rights be limited to individuals or a monolithic understanding of culture, nor should it be used to essentialize the meaning of gender or cultural claims. Although some may be skeptical, it is my view that gendered cultural rights can empower more than they can harm.

This book presents a new way to examine the human rights challenges that arise in the multicultural state and defuse the false conflict between two central human rights. It points towards a future in which the cultural and gender dimensions of rights claims are recognized and, instead of being asked to divest herself of it, a woman truly can invoke her right to culture.

BIBLIOGRAPHY

Aamot-Snapp, Erik W. (1995). When Judicial Flexibility Becomes Abuse of Discretion: Eliminating the "Good Cause" Exception in Indian Child Welfare Act Adoptive Placements. *Minnesota Law Review*, 79(5): 1167-1196.

Aboriginal and Torres Strait Islander Heritage Protection Act (1984). http://scaleplus.law.gov.au/ogi-bin/topic

Aboriginal Legal Rights Movement, Inc. v. The State of South Australia and Iris Eliza Stevens (1995). 64 ASR 551.

Abu-Lughod, L (2002). Do Muslim Women Really Need Saving? Anthropological Reflections on Cultural Relativism and its Others. *American Anthropologist*, 104(3): 783-790.

Adams, Jill E. (1994). The Indian Child Welfare Act of 1978: Protecting Tribal Interests in a Land of Individual Rights. *American Indian Law Review*, 19(2): 301-351.

Ahmed, Leila (1972). *Women and Gender in Islam: Historical Roots of a Modern Debate*. New Haven: Yale University Press

Albaugh, Diane (1991). Tribal Jurisdiction over Indian Children: Mississippi Band of Choctaw Indians v. Holyfield. *American Indian Law Review*, 16(2): 533-558.

al-Hibri, Azizah Y. (1997). Deconstructing Patriarchal Jurisprudence in Islamic Law: A Faithful Approach. In Adrien Katherine Wing (Ed.) (2000). *Global Critical Race Feminism: An International Reader*. New York: New York University Press, pp. 221-233.

al-Hibri, Azizah Y. (1997). Islam, Law, and Custom: Redefining Muslim Women's Rights. *American University Journal of International Law and Policy*, 12(1): 1-45.

Alston, Philip and Steiner, Henry J. (Eds.) (1996). *International Human Rights in Context: Law, Politics, Morals,* Oxford: Clarendon Press, pp. 887-967.

Andersen, Eric G. (1998). Children, Parents, and Non-parents: Protected Interests and Legal Standards. *Brigham Young University Law Review*, p. 935-1002.

An-Na'im, A. (2000). Human Rights and Islamic Identity in France and Uzbekistan: Mediation of the Local and the Global. *Human Rights Quarterly*, 22(4): 906-941.

Askin, Kelly D. and Dorean Koenig (Eds.) (1999). *Women and International Human Rights Law*. Ardsley, NY: Transnational Publishers.

111

Avitzur v. Avitzur, Court of Appeals of New York (1983), 58 NY 2d 108 1983.

Baines, Cynthia DeBula (1996). L'Affaire des Foulards—Discrimination, or the Price of a Secular Public Educational System. *Vanderbilt Journal of Transnational Law*, 29: 303-327.

Bakesis, Christine D. (1996). The Indian Child Welfare Act of 1978: Violating Personal Rights for the Sake of the Tribe. *Notre Dame Journal of Law, Ethics & Public Policy*, 10(2): 543-586.

Baron, Roger M. (1991). The Resurgence of the "Tribal Interest" in Indian Child Custody Proceedings. *Tulsa Law Journal*, 26(3): 315-346.

Bell, Diane (1999). *Ngarrindjeri Wurruwarrin: A World that Is, Was and Will Be*. North Melbourne, Vic.: BRAD.

Benhabib, Seyla (1999). "Nous" et "les Autres": The Politics of Complex Cultural Dialogue in a Global Civilization. In Christian Joppke and Steven Lukes (Eds.). *Multicultural Questions*. Oxford: Oxford University Press, pp. 44-64.

Bennett, Gordon (1978). *Aboriginal Rights in International Law*. London: Anthropological Institute [for] Survival International.

Bennett, Michele K. (1993). Native American Children: Caught in the Web of the Indian Child Welfare Act. *Hamline Law Review*, 16(3): 953-973.

Beriss, David (1990). Scarves, Schools, and Segregation: The *Foulard* Affair. *French Politics & Society*, 8(1): 1-13.

Bloul, R.A. (1996). Victims or Offenders? 'Other' Women in French Sexual Politics. *European Journal of Women's Studies*, 3(3): 251-270.

Bourke, Joanna (1997). Women's Business: Sex, Secrets and the Hindmarsh Island Affair. *UNSW Law Journal*, 20(2): 333-351.

Bowen, John R. (2007). *Why the French Don't Like Headscarves: Islam, the State, and Public Space*. Oxford; Princeton: Princeton University Press.

Brandt, Michele and Jeffrey A. Kaplan (1995). The Tension between Women's Rights and Religious Rights: Reservations to CEDAW by Egypt, Bangladesh, and Tunisia. *Journal of Law and Religion*, 12(1): 105-142.

Brechon, P. and Mitra, S. K. (1992). The National Front in France—The Emergence of an Extreme Right Protest Movement. *Comparative Politics*, 25(1): 63-82.

Brems, Eva (1997). Enemies or Allies? Feminism and Cultural Relativism as Dissident Voices in Human Rights Discourse. *Human Rights Quarterly*, 19: 136-164.

Brennan, Frank (1993). Mabo and the Racial Discrimination Act: The Limits of Native Title and Fiduciary Duty under Australia's Sovereign Parliaments. *Sydney Law Review*, 15(2): 206-222.

Breu, M. and Marchese, R. (2000). Social Commentary and Political Action: The Headscarf as Popular Culture and Symbol of Political Confrontation in Modern Turkey. *Journal of Popular Culture*, 33(4): 25-38.

Brownlie, Ian (1992). *Treaties and Indigenous Peoples*. Oxford: Clarendon Press; New York: Oxford University Press.

Broyde, Michael J. (2001). *Marriage, Divorce and the Abandoned Wife in Jewish Law: A Conceptual Understanding of the Agunah Problems in America*. Hoboken, NJ: Ktav Publishing House.

Brozan, Nadine (1998). Rabbis Stir Furor by Helping "Chained Women" to Leave Husbands. *The New York Times* Aug. 13, 1998: B1.

Bunch, Charlotte (1995). Transforming Human Rights from a Feminist Perspective. In Julie Peters and Andrea Wolper (Eds.), *Women's Rights Human Rights: International Feminist Perspectives* (pp. 11-17). New York: Routledge.

Bunch, Charlotte (1990). Women's Rights as Human Rights: Toward a Re-Vision of Human Rights. *Human Rights Quarterly*, 12(4): 486-498.

Byrnes, Andrew (1989). The "Other" Human Rights Treaty Body: The Work of the Committee on the Elimination of Discrimination Against Women. *The Yale Journal of International Law*, 14(1).

Byrnes, Andrew (1994). Toward More Effective Enforcement of Women's Human Rights Through the Use of International Human Rights Law and Procedures. In Rebecca J. Cook (Ed.), *Human Rights of Women: National and International Perspectives* (pp. 189-227). Philadelphia: University of Pennsylvania Press.

Caldwell, Paulette M. A Hair Piece: Perspectives on the Intersection of Race and Gender. In Adrien Katherine Wing (Ed.) (1997). *Critical Race Feminism: A Reader*. New York: New York University Press. pp. 297-305.

Capotorti, Francesco (1977). *Study on the Rights of Persons Belonging to Ethnic, Religious, and Linguistic Minorities*. New York: United Nations. UN Document E/CN.4/Sub.2/384/Add.1-7 (1977).

Chapman and Others v. Minister for Aboriginal and Torres Strait Islander Affairs and Others; Barton and Another v. Minister for Aboriginal and Torres Strait Islander Affairs and Others (1995). 133 *ALR*, 74.

Carriere, Jeanne Louise (1994). Representing the Native American: Culture, Jurisdiction, and the Indian Child Welfare Act. *Iowa Law Review*, 79(3):585-652.

Charlesworth, Hilary; Chinkin, Christine; Wright, Shelley (1991). Feminist Approaches to International Law. *American Journal of International Law*, 85(4): 613-645.

Charlesworth, Hilary (1994). What are "Women's International Human Rights"? In Rebecca J. Cook (Ed.). *Human Rights of Women: National and International Perspectives.* Philadelphia: University of Penn. Press, pp. 58-84.

Committee on the Elimination of All Forms against Women. *General Recommendation 19 (A/47/38).* United Nations.

Connelly, Michael E. (1993). Tribal Jurisdiction under Section 1911(b) of the Indian Child Welfare Act of 1978: Are the States Respecting Indian Sovereignty? *New Mexico Law Review,* 23(2): 479-497.

Cook, Rebecca J. (Ed.) (1994). *Human Rights of Women: National and International Perspectives.* Philadelphia: University of Pennsylvania Press.

Crenshaw, Kimberlé Williams. Mapping the Margins: Intersectionality, Identity Politics, and Violence against Women of Color. In Kimberlé Crenshaw et al. (Eds.). *Critical Race Theory: The Key Writings that Formed the Movement.* New York: The New Press, pp. 357-383.

Daly, Mary (1978). *Gyn/ecology: The Metaethics of Radical Feminism.* Boston: Beacon Press.

Davis, Toni Hahn (1993). The Existing Indian Family Exception to the Indian Child Welfare Act. *American Journal of Family Law,* 7(4): 189-206.

Deveaux, Monique (2000). *Cultural Pluralism and the Dilemmas of Justice.* Ithaca, NY: Cornell University Press.

Deveaux, Monique (2006). *Gender and Justice in Multicultural Liberal States.* Oxford: Oxford University Press.

Domestic Relations Law Article 13. Provisions Applicable to more than one type of matrimonial action. NY CLS Rel § 253 (2004).

Dornin, Tim (Oct. 27, 1999). SA: Court Rules against Fresh Bid to Stop Hindmarsh Bridge. AAP NEWSFEED.

Driessen, Geert and Van der Slik, Frans (2001). Religion, Denomination, and Education in the Netherlands: Cognitive and Noncognitive Outcomes After an Era of Secularization. *Journal for the Scientific Study of Religion,* 40(4): 561-572.

Dussel, Ines (2001). What Can Multiculturalism Tell Us about Difference? The Reception of Multicultural Discourses in France and Argentina. In Carl A. Grant and Joy L. Lei (Eds.) (2001). *Global Constructions of Multicultural Education: Theories and Realities,* Mahwah, NJ: Lawrence Erlbaum Associates, pp. 93-114.

Dworkin, Andrea (1987). *Intercourse.* New York: The Free Press.

Dworkin, Andrea (1999). *Letters from a Warzone.* New York: Lawrence Hill Books.

Dworkin, Andrea (1997). *Life and Death.* New York; London; Toronto; Sydney; Singapore: The Free Press.

Estin, Ann Laquer. Embracing Tradition: Pluralism in American Family Law. *Maryland Family Law* 63: 540-604.

Feldblum, Miriam (1993). Paradoxes of Ethnic Politics—the Case of France—Maghrebis in France. *Ethnic and Racial Studies*, 16(1): 52-74.

Feldman, Marc (1990). Jewish Divorce and Secular Courts: Helping a Jewish Woman Obtain a Get. *Berkeley Women's Law Journal* v.5: 139-169.

Fergie, Deane (1996). Secret Envelopes and Inferential Tautologies. *Journal of Australian Studies*, 48: 13-24.

Fisher, Elizabeth Mary (1996). Subservience, Concealment and Impudence. *Journal of Australian Studies*, 48: 52-57.

Galeotti, Anna Elisabeth (1993). Citizenship and Equality: The Place for Toleration," *Political Theory*, 21(4): 585-605.

Gallagher, Brian D. (1994). Indian Child Welfare Act of 1978: The Congressional Foray into the Adoption Process. *Northern Illinois University Law Review*, 15(1): 81-106.

Gelder, Ken and Jacobs, Jane M. (1995). "Talking out of Place": Authorizing the Aboriginal Sacred in Postcolonial Australia. *Cultural Studies*, 9(1): 150-160.

Giahn v. Giahn, Supreme Court of N.Y., App. Div., April 4. 2000 (unreported).

Goldberg-Ambrose, Carole (1994). Heeding the 'Voice' of Tribal Law in Indian Child Welfare Proceedings. In René Kuppe and Richard Potz (Eds.) (1994). *Law and Anthropology: International Yearbook for Legal Anthropology*, vol. 7. Dordrecht; Boston; London: Martinus Nijhoff Publishers.

Graham, Lorie M. (1998). "The Past Never Vanishes:" A Contextual Critique of the Existing Indian Family Doctrine. *American Indian Law Review*, 23(1): 2-52.

Green, December (1999). *Gender Violence in Africa: African Women's Responses*. New York: St. Martin's Press.

Greenawalt, Kent (1998). "Religious Law and Civil Law: Using Secular Law to Assure Observance of Practices with Religious Significance." *Southern California Law Review* 71: 781-843.

Greenberg-Korbin, Michelle (1999). "Civil Enforceability of Religious Prenuptial Agreements." *Columbia Journal of Law and Social Problems* 32: 359-397.

Griffiths, Anne (2001). Gendering Culture: Towards a Plural Perspective on Kwena Women's Rights. In Jane K. Cowan et al. (2001). *Culture and Rights: Anthropological Perspectives*. Cambridge: Cambridge University Press.

Hancock, Nathan (1996). Disclosure in the Public Interest? Is Full Disclosure of Secrets Required by Current Heritage Legislation? *Alternative Law Journal*, 21(1): 19-23.

Hancock, Nathan (1995). How to Keep a Secret: Building Bridges between Two "Laws". *Aboriginal Law Bulletin*, 2(77): 4-9.

Hargreaves, Alec G. (1995). *Immigration, "Race," and Ethnicity in Contemporary France*. London; New York: Rutledge.

Hemming, Steve (1996). Inventing Ethnography. *Journal of Australian Studies*, 25-39.

Herz, Richard (1993). Legal Protection for Indigenous Cultures: Sacred Sites and Communal Rights. *Virginia Law Review*, 79(3): 691-716.

High Court to Weigh Custody of Twins (June 2, 1988). *The New York Times*, section C, p. 13, column 3.

Hocking, Barbara (1993). Aboriginal Law Does Now Run in Australia: Reflections on the Mabo Case: From *Cooper v. Stuart* through *Milirrpum* to *Mabo*. *Sydney Law Review*, 15(2): 187-205.

Hollinger, Joan Heifetz (1996). The Uniform Adoption Act. *Family Law Quarterly*, 30(2): 345-378.

Holt, Marilyn Irvin (2001). *Indian Orphanages*. Lawrence, Kansas: University Press of Kansas.

Holyfield v. Choctaw Social Services/Mississippi Band of Choctaw Indians, The Natural Mother and Alleged Natural Father, No. AD 017-90. (Mississippi Band of Choctaw Indians Tribal Court, July 27, 1990, recorded in Adoption Book a, p. 89-90.

Howland, Courtney (Ed.) (1999). *Religious Fundamentalism and the Human Rights of Women*. New York: Palgrave.

Human Rights Committee (1994). *General Comment No. 23: The Rights of Minorities (Art. 27): 08/04/94*. Geneva, Switzerland: United Nations. CCPR/C21/Rev.1/Add.5.

In re Baby Boy L (1993). 24 Cal. App. 4th 596.

In re Bridget R. (1996). 41 Cal App. 4th 1483, 49 Cal.Rptr.2d 507.

In re Wanomi P. (1989). 216 Cal. App. 3d 156, 264 Cal.Rptr. 623.

In the Matter of B.B. and G.B., Minors; Mississippi Band of Choctaw Indians v. Holyfield (1987). 511 So. 2d 918.

Jacob, Marvin E. (1995). "The Agunah Problem and the So-Called New York State Get Law: A Legal and Halachic Analysis." In Jack Nusan Porter (Ed.) (1995). *Women in Chains: A Sourcebook on the Agunah*. Northvale, NJ: Jason Aronson Inc., pp. 159-184.

Jacobs, Jane M. (1993). "Shake 'im this Country": The Mapping of the Aboriginal Sacred in Australia—The Case of Coronation Hill. In Peter Jackson and Jan Penrose (Eds.) (1993). *Constructions of Race, Place and Nation,* London: UCL Press, pp. 100-120.

Jagger, Alison M. (1998). Globalizing Feminist Ethics. *Hypatia.* 13(2): 7-31.

Johnson, Troy R. (Ed.) (1991). *The Indian Child Welfare Act: The Next Ten Years: Indian Homes for Indian Children: Conference Proceedings of the American Indian Studies Center.* Los Angeles, CA: American Indian Studies Center, UCLA.

Jones, B. J. (1995). *The Indian Child Welfare Act Handbook: A Legal Guide to the Custody and Adoption of Native American Children.* Chicago: Section of Family Law, American Bar Association.

Kahan, Linda S. Jewish Divorce and Secular Courts: The Promise of *Avitzur. The Georgetown Law Journal* 73: 193-224.

Doreen Kartinyeri and Anor v The Commonwealth of Australia (1998). 152 ALR 540.

Keck, Margaret J. and Kathryn Sikkink (1998). *Activists Beyond Borders: Advocacy Networks in International Politics.* Ithaca, New York: Cornell University Press.

Keen, Ian (1993). Aboriginal Beliefs vs. Mining at Coronation Hill: The Containing Force of Traditionalism. *Human Organization,* 52(4): 344-355.

Kerruishi, Valerie (1999). Bridging the Cultural Gap on Hindmarsh Island: Review of *Ngarrindjeri Wurruwarrin: A World that Is, Was and Will Be* by Diane Bell. *Law Society Journal,* 37(2): 103.

Ko, Dorothy (2005). *Cinderella's Sisters: A Revisionist History of Footbinding.* Berkeley; Los Angeles: University of California Press.

Koker, L. (1996). Political Toleration as Politics of Recognition—The Headscarves Affair Revisited. *Political Theory* 24(2): 315-320.

Kukathas, Chandran (1992). Are There any Cultural Rights? *Political Theory,* 20(1): 105-139.

Kukathas, Chandran (1997). Cultural Toleration. In Ian Shapiro and Will Kymlicka (Eds.) (1997). *Ethnicity and Group Rights.* New York; London: New York University Press, pp. 69-104.

Kymlicka, Will (2001). *Politics in the Vernacular: Nationalism, Multiculturalism and Citizenship.* Oxford: Oxford University Press.

Kymlicka, Will (1999). Comments on Shachar and Spinner-Halev: An Update from the Multiculturalism Wars. In Christian Joppke and Steven Lukes (Eds.). *Multicultural Questions.* Oxford: Oxford University Press, pp. 112-132.

Kymlicka, Will (1995). *Multicultural Citizenship: A Liberal Theory of Minority Rights.* Oxford: Clarendon Press.

Langton, Marcia (1996). The Hindmarsh Island Bridge Affair: How Aboriginal Women's Religion became an Administrable Affair. *Australian Feminist Studies*, 11(24): 211-217.

Lapeyronnie, D (1987). Assimilation Mobilization and Collective Action among Maghreb Immigrants' Children in France. *Revue Francaise de Sociologie*, 28(2): 287-318.

Lieberman, Elizabeth (1983). *Avitzur v. Avitzur*: The Constitutional Implications of Judicially Enforcing Religious Agreements. *The Catholic University Law Review* 33: 219-243.

Limage, L. J. (2000). Education and Muslim Identity: The Case of France. *Comparative Education*, 36(1): 73-94.

Sandra Lovelace v. Canada. Communication No. R.6/24. Views of the Human Rights Committee. Report of the Human Rights Committee, Annex XVIII. General Assembly Official Records, 36th Session, Supplement No. 40 (A/36/40). New York: United Nations, 1981.

MacKinnon, Catherine A. (1987). *Feminism Unmodified: Discourses on Life and Law*. Cambridge, MA; London: Harvard University Press.

Maddock, Kenneth (1991). Metamorphosing the Sacred in Australia. *The Australian Journal of Anthropology*, 2(2): 213-232.

Mahmood, Tahir. Interaction of Islam and Public Law in Independent India. In R. S. Khare (Ed.) (1999). *Perspectives on Islamic Law, Justice, and Society*. Lanham; Boulder; New York; Oxford: Rowman & Littlefield Publishers, Inc.

Maier, Silvia (2001). Multicultural Jurisprudence: A Study of the Legal Recognition of Cultural Minority Rights in France and Germany. Doctoral Dissertation, University of Southern California.

Margolick, David (1983). "Court Rules New York Can Enforce Jewish Marriage Contract." *The New York Times*, Feb. 16, 1983, B1.

Marshall, Lawrence (1986). The Religion Clauses and Compelled Religious Divorces: A Study in Marital and Constitutional Separations. *Northwestern University Law Review* 80(1): 204-258.

McGoldrick, Dominic (2006). *Human Rights and Religion: The Islamic Headscarf Debate in Europe*. Oxford; Portland, OR: Hart.

McGoldrick, Dominic (1991). Canadian Indians, Cultural Rights and the Human Rights Committee. *International and Comparative Law Quarterly*, 40: 658-669.

Mernissi, Fatima (1975). *Beyond the Veil: Male-Female Dynamics in Modern Muslim Society*. Bloomington, Indiana; Indianapolis: Indiana University Press.

Merry, Sally (2006). *Human Rights and Gender Violence*. Chicago: University of Chicago Press.

Miller, Jessica Davidson (1997). The History of the Agunah in America: A Clash of Religious Law and Social Progress. *Women's Rights Law Reporter* 19: 1-15.

Minkin v. Minkin (1981). 180 New Jersey Super. 260, 434 A.2d 665.

Minow, Martha (1991). Identities. *Yale Journal of Law and the Humanities,* 3(1): 97-130.

Mir-Hosseini, Ziba (1999). *Islam and Gender: The Religious Debate in Contemporary Iran.* Princeton, NJ: Princeton University Press.

Mississippi Band of Choctaw Indians v. Holyfield (1989). 490 U.S. 30, 109 S. Ct. 1597, 104 L. Ed. 2d 29.

Morsink, Johannes (1991). Women's Rights in the Universal Declaration. *Human Rights Quarterly.* 13(2): 229-256.

Moruzzi, Norma Claire (1994). A Problem with Headscarves—Contemporary Complexities of Political and Social Identity. *Political Theory,* 22(4): 653-672.

Muir, Kathie (1996). Media Representations of Ngarrindjeri Women. *Journal of Australian Studies,* 48: 73-82.

Mullally, Siobhan (2006). *Gender, Culture and Human Rights: Reclaiming Universalism.* Oxford; Portland, Oregon: Hart.

Muslim Pupils Will Take Off Scarfs in Class. *Los Angeles Times,* Dec. 3, 1987, A15.

Narayan, Uma (1998). Essence of Culture and a Sense of History: A Feminist Critique of Cultural Essentialism. *Hypatia,* 13(2): 86-106.

Nesiah, Vasuki (1993). Toward a Feminist Internationality: A Critique of U.S. Legal Scholarship. In Adrien Katherine Wing (Ed.) (2000). *Global Critical Race Feminism: An International Reader.* New York: New York University Press, pp. 42-52.

Nettheim, Garth (1996). Women's business and law. *Aboriginal Law Bulletin,* 3(80): 24.

Nettheim, Garth (1993). "The Consent of the Natives": Mabo and indigenous political rights. *Sydney Law Review,* 15(2): 223-246.

Nicholls, Christine (1996). Literacy and gender. *Journal of Australian Studies,* 48: 59-72.

Nixon, Sherrill (Dec. 13, 1999). SA: Hindmarsh Island Bridge Case in Court. AAP NEWSFEED.

Nixon, Sherrill (Nov. 16, 1999). SA: Overseas Bid to Stop Hindmarsh Bridge. AAP NEWSFEED.

Norvill and Another v. Chapman and Others; Norvill and Another v. Barton and Others; Tickner v Chapman and Others; Tickner v. Barton and Others (1995). 133 ALR, 226.

Nowak, Manfred (1993). *UN Convention on Civil and Political Rights: CCPR Commentary*. Arlington, Virginia: N.P. Engel.

Null, David (1985). The Indian Child Welfare Act. *Journal of Juvenile Law*, 9(2): 391-400.

Obiora, Leslye Ameda (1997). Bridges and Barricades: Rethinking Polemics and Intransigence in the Campaign against Female Circumcision. In Adrien Katherine Wing (Ed.) (2000). *Global Critical Race Feminism*, pp. 260-274.

Okin, Susan Moller (2002). "Mistresses of Their Own Destiny": Group Rights, Gender, and Realistic Rights of Exit. *Ethics*, 112(2): 205-230.

Okin, Susan Moller (1999). *Is Multiculturalism Bad for Women?* Princeton, NJ: Princeton University Press.

Okin, Susan Moller (1998). Feminism and Multiculturalism: Some Tensions. *Ethics*, 108(4): 661-684.

Okin, Susan Moller (1998). Feminism, Women's Human Rights, and Cultural Differences. *Hypatia*, 13(2): 32-52.

Oloka-Onyango, J. and Tamale, Sylvia (1995). "The Personal is Political," or Why Women's Rights are Indeed Human Rights: An African Perspective on International Feminism. *Human Rights Quarterly*, 17(4):691-731.

Otto, Dianne (2002). "Gender Comment:" Why Does the UN Committee on Economic, Social, and Cultural Rights need a General Comment on Women? *Canadian Journal of Women and the Law*, 14: 1-52.

Packer, Corinne (2003). African Women, Traditions, and Human Rights: A Critical Analysis of Contemporary 'Universal' Discourses and Approaches. In David P. Forsythe and Patrice C. McMahon (Eds.). *Human Rights and Diversity: Area Studies Revisited*. Pp. 159-181.

Parekh, Bhikhu (2000). *Rethinking Multiculturalism: Cultural Diversity and Political Theory*. Cambridge, Mass.: Harvard University Press.

Patwari, M. I. (1990-1991). Human Rights in Islamic Law and International Law: A Comparison. *Islamic and Comparative Law Quarterly*, 9091 (1011): 17-28.

Peach, Ceri and Günther Glebe (1995). Muslim Minorities in Western Europe. *Ethnic and Racial Studies*, 18(1): 26-45.

Pengelley, Nicholas (1998). Before the High Court: the Hindmarsh Island Bridge Act. (Must laws based on the race power be for the "benefit" of Aborigines and Torres Strait Islanders? And what has bridge building got to do with the race power anyway?), *Sydney Law Review*, 20(1): 144-157.

Perl v. Perl (1987). 512 N.Y.S.2d 372, 126 A.D.2d 91.

Perry, Twila L. (1993-1994). The transracial adoption controversy: an analysis of discourse and subordination. *New York University Review of Law and Social Change*, 21(1): 33-108.

Peters, Julie and Andrea Wolper (Eds.) (1995). *Women's Rights/Human Rights: International Feminist Perspectives*. New York: Routledge.

Poulter, Sebastian (1997). Muslim Headscarves in School: Contrasting Legal Approaches in England and France. *Oxford Journal of Legal Studies*, 17(1): 43-74.

Poulter, Sebastian (1995). Multiculturalism and Human Rights for Muslim Families in English Law. In Michael King (Ed.) *God's Law Versus State Law: Construction of an Islamic Identity in Western Europe*. London: Grey Seal Books, pp. 81-87.

Poulter, Sebastian (1987). Ethnic Minority Customs, English Law and Human Rights. *The International and Comparative Law Quarterly*, 36: 589-615.

Pui-lan, Kwok (2002). Unbinding Our Feet: Saving Brown Women and Feminist Religious Discourse. In Laura E. Donaldson and Kwok Pui-lan (Eds.) (2002). *Postcolonialism, Feminism, and Religious Discourse*. New York: Routlege, pp. 62-81.

Reanda, Laura (1981). Human Rights and Women's Rights: The United Nations Approach. *Human Rights Quarterly*, 3(2): 11-31.

Renteln, Alison Dundes (2004). *The Cultural Defense*. New York: Oxford University Press.

Renteln, Alison Dundes (2004). Visual Religious Symbols to the Law. *American Behavioral Scientist* 47(12): 1573-1596.

Riles, Annelise (2000). *The Network Inside Out*. Ann Arbor: University of Michigan Press.

Riskin, Shlomo (1989). *Women and Jewish Divorce: The Rebellious Wife, the Agunah and the Right of Women to Initiate Divorce in Jewish Law, A Halckhic Solution*. Hoboken, NJ: Ktav Publishing House.

Ritchie, David (1994). Principles and Practice of Site Protection Laws in Australia. In David L. Carmichael, Jane Hubert, Brian Reeves and Audhild Schanche (Eds.) (1994). *Sacred Sites, Sacred Places*. London; New York: Routledge, 227-244.

Romany, Celina. Themes for a Conversation on Race and Gender in International Human Rights Law. In Adrien Katherine Wing (Ed.) (2000). *Global Critical Race Feminism: An International Reader*. New York: New York University Press, pp. 53-66.

Rostain, Tanina (1987). Permissible Accommodations of Religion: Reconsidering the New York *Get* Statute. *The Yale Law Journal* 96: 1147-1171.

Rowell, Meredith (1983). Women and Land Claims in the Northern Territory. In Nicolas Peterson and Marcia Langton (Eds.) (1983). *Aborigines, Land and Land Rights*, Canberra: Australian Institute of Aboriginal Studies.

Rozario, S. (1998). On Being Australian and Muslim: Muslim Women as Defenders of Islamic heritage. *Women's Studies International Forum*, 21(6): 649-661.

Ryan, Lyndall (1996). Origins of a Royal Commission. *Journal of Australian Studies*, 48: 1-12.

SA: Crane Protest at Bridge Construction Site (Dec. 8, 1999). AAP NEWS-FEED.

Saas, C. (2001). Muslim Headscarf and Secularism in France. *European Journal of Migration Law*, (3-4): 453-456.

Sabbah, Fatna (1984). Lakeland, Mary Jo (Trans.) *Woman in the Muslim Unconscious.* New York; Oxford; Toronto; Sydney; Paris; Frankfurt: Pergamon Press.

Santa Clara Pueblo v. Martinez (1978). 436 U.S. 49.

Savery, Lyn (2007). *Engendering the State: The International Diffusion of Women's Human Rights.* Routledge.

Scales-Trent, Judy (1999). African Women in France: Immigration, Family, and Work. *Brooklyn Journal of International Law*, 24: 705+.

Schwartz v. Schwartz. 153 Misc.2d 789 (1992), on appeal, 235 A.D.2d 468 (1997).

Senate Indian Affairs and House Resources Comittees (June 18, 1997). Testimony of Thomas L. Leclaire, Director of the Office of Tribal Justice, Department of Justice. www.senate.gov/~scia/hearings/818_doj.htm.

Shachar, Ayelet (2001). *Multicultural Jurisdictions: Cultural Differences and Women's Rights.* Cambridge: Cambridge University Press.

Shachar, Ayelet (1999). The Paradox of Multicultural Vulnerability. In Christian Joppke and Steven Lukes (Eds.). *Multicultural Questions.* Oxford: Oxford University Press, pp. 87-111.

Shachar, Ayelet (Summer 2000). The Puzzle of Interlocking Power Hierarchies: Sharing the Pieces of Jurisdictional Authority. *Harvard Civil Rights-Civil Liberties Law Review* 35: 385-426.

Singh, B. R. (1999). Responses of Liberal Democratic Societies to Claims from Ethnic Minorities to Community Rights. *Educational Studies*, 25(2): 187-204.

Slaughter, M. M. (2000). Contested Identities: The Adoption of Indian Children and the Liberal State. *Sociology Legal Studies*, 9(2): 227-248.

Song, Sarah (2007). *Justice, Gender, and the Politics of Multiculturalism.* Cambridge; New York: Cambridge University Press.

South Australia Parliament (1997). *Hindmarsh Island Bridge Act*, No. 60 of 1997. Assented to 22 May 1997.

Spiliopoulou Akermark, Athanasia (1997). *Justifications of Minority Protection in International Law.* London; Boston: Kluwer Law International.

Spinner-Halev, Jeff (1999). Cultural Pluralism and Partial Citizenship. In Christian Joppke and Steven Lukes (Eds.). *Multicultural Questions*. Oxford: Oxford University Press, pp. 65-86.

Stamatopoulou, Elsa (2007). *Cultural Rights in International Law: Article 27 of the Universal Declaration of Human Rights and Beyond*. Leiden: Martinus Nifjhoff Publishers.

Stuart, Amy (1997). Review: *Secret Women's Business: The Hindmarsh Island affair* (Lyndall Ryan (ed.)). *Australian Feminist Studies*, 12(26): 357-358.

Tager, Esther (1999). The Chained Wife. *Netherlands Quarterly of Human Rights,* 17(4): 425-457.

Tahzib, Bahiyyih (1996). *Freedom of Religion or Belief: Ensuring Effective International Legal Protection*. The Hague; Boston: Nijhoff.

Tahzib-Lie, Bahia (2000). Applying a Gender Perspective in the Area of the Right to Freedom of Religion or Belief. *Brigham Young University Law Review*, 967-987.

Taylor, Richard B. (1991). Curbing the Erosion of Rights of Native Americans: Was the Supreme Court Successful in *Mississippi Band of Choctaw Indians v. Holyfield*? *Journal of Family Law*, 29(1): 171-189.

Tehan, Maureen (1996). A Tale of Two Cultures. *Alternative Law Journal*, 21(1): 10-14.

Tergel, Alf (1998). *Human Rights in Cultural and Religious Traditions*. Uppsala Publishing.

Terray, Emmanuel (2004). Headscarf Hysteria. *The New Left Review* 26: 118-127.

Thierry, X. (2001). Foreign Immigrants to France, 1994-1999. *Population*, 56(3): 423-450.

Thornberry, Patrick (1991). *International Law and Rights of Minorities*. Oxford; New York: Oxford University Press.

Tohidi, Nayereh (1996). Soviet in Public, Azeri in Private: Gender, Islam, and Nationality in Soviet and Post-Soviet Azerbaijan. *Women's Studies International Forum*, 19(1/2): 111-123.

Tonkinson, Robert (1997). Anthropology and Aboriginal Tradition: The Hindmarsh Island Bridge Affair and the Politics of Interpretation. *Oceania*, 68(1): 1-26.

United Nations (1966). International Covenant on Civil and Political Rights. In Ian Brownlie (Ed) (1995). *Basic Documents in International Law, 4th ed.* Oxford: Clarendon Press, pp. 276-297.

United Nations (1966). International Covenant on Economic, Social and Cultural Rights. In Ian Brownlie (Ed.) (1995). *Basic Documents in International Law, 4th ed.* Oxford: Clarendon Press, pp. 263-275.

United Nations (1989). *Convention on the Rights of the Child.* Adopted by the General Assembly November 20, 1989. Entered into force on September 2, 1990.

Uren, Kate (November 14, 2000). Tickner Finds out Why He Imposed Ban. *The Advertiser*, p. 5.

Valdes, Franscisco, et al. (2002). *Crossroads, Directions, and a New Critical Race Theory.* Philadelphia: Temple University Press.

van Bijsterveld, Sophie C. (2000). Religion, International Law and Policy in the Wider European Arena: New Dimensions and Developments. In Rex J. Ahdar (Ed.) *Law and Religion.* Burlington, VT: Ashgate, pp. 163-180.

van Velsen, J. (1967). The Extended-case Method and Situational Analysis. In A. L. Epstein (Ed.), *The Craft of Social Anthropology.* London: Tanstock, pp. 129-149.

Viorst, Milton (1996). The Muslims of France. *Foreign Affairs*, pp. 78-96.

Volpp, Leti (2001). Feminism v. Multiculturalism. *Columbia Law Review* 101: 1181-1218.

Vonk, M. E. (2001). Cultural Competence for Transracial Adoptive Parents. *Social Work*, 46(3): 246-255.

Waldron, Jeremy (1995). Minority Cultures and the Cosmopolitan Alternative. In Will Kymlicka (Ed.) (1995). *The Rights of Minority Cultures.* New York: Oxford University Press, pp. 93-119.

Watts, Stan (1989). Voluntary Adoptions under the Indian Child Welfare Act of 1978: Balancing the Interests of Children, Families, and Tribes. *Southern California Law Review*, 63(1): 213-256.

Wayland, Sarah V (1997). Religious Expression in Public Schools: Kirpans in Canada, Hijab in France. *Ethnic and Racial Studies*, 20(3): 545-561.

Weissbrodt David and Connie de la Vega (2007). *International Human Rights Law: An Introduction.* Philadelphia: University of Pennsylvania Press.

Weiner, James F. (1999). Culture in a Sealed Envelope: The Concealment of Australian Aboriginal Heritage and Tradition in the Hindmarsh Island Bridge Affair. *The Journal of the Royal Anthropological Institute*, 5(2): 193-210.

Weiner, James F. (1997). Must our Informants Mean What they Say? *Canberra Anthropology*, 20(1 and 2): 82-95.

Wihtol de Wenden, Catherine (1998). Young Muslim Women in France: Cultural and Psychological Adjustments. *Political Psychology*, 19(1):133-146.

Wilson and Ors v. The Minister for Aboriginal and Torres Strait Islander Affairs and Anor. (1996). 189 CLR 1.

Woodhouse, Barbara Bennett (1995). "Are You My Mother?": Conceptualizing Children's Identity Rights in Transracial Adoptions. *Duke Journal of Gender, Law & Policy*, 2: 107-129.

Wunder, John R. (Ed.) (1996). *Native Americans and the Law: Contemporary and Historical Perspectives on American Indian Rights, Freedoms, and Sovereignty*. New York; London: Garland Publishing.

ABOUT THE AUTHOR

LINDA VEAZEY is currently an Assistant Professor of Political Science and Coordinator of the Women's and Gender Studies Program at Midwestern State University, in Texas. She received her M.A. and Ph.D. in Political Science from the University of Southern California, with her B.A. in Political Science earned from the University of Montevallo, in Alabama. Dr. Veazey is also a member of the Board of Directors of Amnesty International USA. She and her family reside in Wichita Falls, Texas.

qp

Visit us at *www.quidprobooks.com*.

9 781610 273145